ADOPTION: CHOOSING IT, LIVING IT, LOVING IT

adoption

Choosing It, Living It, Loving It

Straight Answers to Heartfelt Questions

DR. RAY GUARENDI

SERVANT
BOOKS

PUBLISHED BY FRANCISCAN MEDIA
Cincinnati, Ohio

Cover design by Candle Light Studios
Cover photo © Corbis/Sean Justice
Book design by Mark Sullivan

LIBRARY OF CONGRESS CATALOGING-IN-PUBLICATION DATA
Guarendi, Raymond.
Adoption : choosing it, living it, loving it / Ray Guarendi.
p. cm.
Includes bibliographical references.
ISBN 978-0-86716-913-3 (pbk. : alk. paper) 1. Adoption. 2. Adoption—
Psychological aspects. I. Title.
HV875.G83 2009
362.734—dc22

2008046631

ISBN 978-0-86716-913-3

Published by Servant Books, an imprint of Franciscan Media
28 W. Liberty St.
Cincinnati, OH 45202
www.FranciscanMedia.org
www.ServantBooks.org

Printed in the United States of America.

Printed on acid-free paper.

12 13 5 4 3 2

: : : contents : : :

"Everybody has a book in them." Bad grammar aside, this is a popular sentiment. Whether reflecting my loquaciousness or not, I had more than one book in me, and they made their way out over a couple of decades. With some uneven parallels to my adoptive parenthood, upon completing each manuscript I firmly pronounced, "No more books. I've written all I can write."

So it is with more than a touch of irony that only a few months after the publication of my no doubt "absolutely last" book, I began writing *Adoption: Choosing It, Living It, Loving It.* Looking back, I realize this book had been sitting quietly in me for some time, pushing ever harder to make itself heard. It's a cliché, but for me this book is a work of the heart. It was written more quickly than any of my others, as the thought drove me, "Maybe some couple will adopt because of something they read here. Maybe some child unknown to me will get a mom, dad, family, brothers, sisters and more."

What follows is a gathering of the most common adoption questions I hear as a father and psychologist. My three aims are these: one, reassure people by dispelling the most unsettling anxieties, misperceptions and myths about adoption; two, persuade those not thinking adoption to think about it, and those thinking to act; three, guide parents after an adoption to a more relaxed, rewarding family for all involved.

Perhaps if my wife and I had read a book like this a few years back, we wouldn't have stopped adopting at ten kids. Then again, maybe we would have, no matter how many books we read. Who knows, though, where you might go with some of this, or where you might stop?

: : : acknowledgments : : :

Most books are written by many people. This one is no exception. While I was the first to put thoughts to paper, many others made these thoughts into a book.

Thank you, Cindy Cavnar, my editor at Servant Books, for knowing the perfect blend of pushing and pulling to make me keep writing. Your guidance, feedback and professionalism are top-notch.

Thank you, Leah Bryant, for endless patience in typing and retyping my often indecipherable handwritten drafts.

Thank you, Wendy's restaurant. To visit my daughter Sarah, your employee, and to find more quiet than is in our house, I spent many hours writing in your dining room. Dave Thomas, Wendy's founder, was an adopted child and a passionate national advocate for adoption. What a fitting place to write about adoption!

Thank you, Randi, for adding some of the better thoughts in this book. Thank you, kids; your love and antics provided no end of book material. Thank you, God, giver of all that is good.

chapter one

PARTLY PERSONAL

Being a psychologist puts one on the receiving end of all kinds of questions about life. Upon discovering what I do for a living, people will warily ask, "Are you analyzing me?" and then offer, "I have a question for you."

My area of specialty is children and families. Couple my profession with being a father of ten adopted children, and the questions—particularly those about adoption—come faster and more frequently.

Despite popular wisdom, it is not necessary to personally live through something before being able to fully understand it or guide another through it. With fair confidence I can assert that I am not a woman, even as sensitive and aware as I strive to be. Yet well over half of those who seek my advice are female, often with questions uniquely female. In fact, taking the "You can't know unless you've lived it" thinking to its logical extreme, I could only counsel middle-aged, married males with no history of legal troubles, violence, alcohol abuse, drug involvement, mental illness, well—you get the idea. My wife says I could work with immature people, though.

That said, at some level lived experience—if it leads to personal growth and not decline—can afford added insights, thoughts, even emotions helpful to another. Thus it seems natural to begin this book by sharing briefly our family's journey into adoption—how it all began and how it unfolded. Much of our experience is common to those who adopt. It is ordinary stuff. Perhaps in its ordinariness will lie its value.

: : :

WHY ADOPTION?

Dear Dr. Ray: I know this is probably a complex question, but why did you and your wife adopt?

—*Simply Interested*

Complex question, simple answer: We wanted a family. Simpler answer: Randi, my wife, told me to. Simplest answer: My accountant said I needed the tax deductions.

OK, the first simple answer is the real one. We wanted a family, and a good-sized one. My desire for fatherhood and Randi's for motherhood, however, were being squeezed by two other parent figures—Father Time and Mother Nature. I was thirty-four and Randi twenty-nine when I came home with the second urologist's opinion: "He gave us a near zero chance of conceiving. If we do, we should hit the afternoon television circuit to publicly share the miracle." Actually his words were not so blunt, but the truth was.

Sertoli cell–only syndrome was the fancy medical name for my infertility. My grandmother was pleased that at least it was Italian. Sertoli cell–only syndrome is a congenital disorder—present from my birth—that essentially rendered my body incapable of reproduction. For a few weeks after hearing the news, I toyed with suing my mother, but my attorney advised that the statute of limitations had probably lapsed, so I let Mom off with a warning that it had better not happen again.

Psychologists talk about a phenomenon called "flashbulb memories." These are events or circumstances in a person's life so emotionally charged that they forever leave an impression in the mind. For instance, many over age fifty still see clearly the time and place they first heard of President John Kennedy's assassination. For those a bit younger, a flashbulb image could be of Neil Armstrong's televised moon walk; even younger, maybe Michael Jackson's televised moon walk. While these are shared cultural recollections, almost everyone has unique personal memories vividly seared into his or her consciousness.

To this day I can recreate the scene as I gave my wife the urologist's diagnosis—where I was sitting, where she was sitting, the time of day, all manner of minutiae of the moment. Randi, I suspect, has a similar memory, though she could also probably tell you what we both were wearing.

After some tears, mostly upon prematurely concluding that our dream of a large family would stay a dream, we pondered, "What now?"

Two prime options emerged: One, we could accept our circumstances, hope for a miracle conception and make our talk show debut. That idea was quickly discarded, as getting my wife to agree to a talk show visit would involve a bigger miracle than our conceiving. No, option number two was for us. We would look into adoption. Not the titillating stuff of tabloid television, but the core stuff of a much richer reality.

Even twenty years ago Randi and I never waffled over whether to adopt. The decision to move ahead took all of about six seconds. It wasn't rooted in a sense of altruism or self-sacrifice, not at all. Much of it could be labeled self-motivated. We wanted the daddy-mommy-kids existence. Any children granted us, we've come to understand more fully, are gifts of God, no matter how they are given.

Far less certain than our desire to adopt was the who, the how, the how long, the where. So we unsteadily stepped toward a lot of unknowns, reaching for a family even though it looked at the time that it would be a small one.

Like all good fathers, Father Time has a way of teaching us how wrong we are. Some would say time is God's way of bringing his reality into ours. Eventually we would be given our large family, larger than anything we likely could have conceived in the ten or so child-bearing years left to most people in their thirties.

Put simply, without realizing it back when, we adopted not only to have a family but a big one at that. I'm glad I listened to my wife. And to this day I have to pay little in taxes.

:   :   :

NUMBER, PLEASE?

Dear Dr. Ray: Would you share your reasons for adopting ten children? Why not two—the typical family size? Or four—a big family nowadays? Or twelve? Did you plan your family, or did it just happen over time?

—*Looking to Enlarge Too*

I notice you are asking only about even numbers of children. Is this some subtle fear of the "middle child syndrome"?

In the early days of our adoptions, my wife and I didn't talk numbers. We didn't agree, "Ten is a nice, round, everyday number. How about five androgen Americans and five estrogen

Americans? Let's try to stay metric."

The most we knew was that we'd like a large family. We didn't know yet what "large" meant. As the shrinks would say, we didn't "operationalize" the term. We had the general idea, not the specifics.

Like many trying to adopt, we expected to be limited by logistics —time, finances, legalities and availability of children. We were hoping for one child, maybe two, at the outside three, in our wildest dreams, four. How we actually reached ten I'll speak to in a few pages. Right now let's answer the *why* of ten.

Have you ever heard a childless couple assert something like, "We're not sure we want any children. Given where we are in our lives (insert reasons here: age, career, finances, personality, life goals, comfort, concern for the rain forest), we aren't all that attracted to the idea of kids"? If you're a parent, are you tempted to respond, "You're making an uninformed decision. The full rewards of being a parent are only experienced by being a parent. Your life's priorities will yield to your love for that little person"?

OK, you might not say it so succinctly at the moment—I did work on those sentences for about fifteen minutes. But you get the idea. A person only really knows the joy of kids by having them, not by doing a cost-benefit analysis beforehand. Put another way, a real live child can quickly overcome the negatives one anticipates in the abstract.

Sometimes parents confess rather sheepishly to anxiety over whether they will love a second child as much as the first. Their attachment to the first is so intense that they wonder if they can experience the same emotions again. Of course, time shows them that their worries were groundless. Love multiplies; it doesn't divide.

A year or so after adopting Andrew, our first, we got the urge to try again. Why so soon? As much as we had wanted a child, we had underestimated our reaction to him. Parenthood was much more positive than we had foreseen, even with the spit, regurgitation and other body leakage—his, not ours. We felt like toddlers after being bounced on Grandpa's knee until it goes numb: "Do it again." The most indulgent grandparents, though, have a limit.

After our third child, Sarah, we were so grateful to have more kids than expected, we were ready, however reluctantly, to accept our family size. Looking back, three is a number that lends itself to some good lines. I liked watching people's expressions after telling them, "We have three children—one of each."

Fortunately, three wasn't an end: It was a beginning. We stayed open to adoptions, and the adoptions stayed open to us.

After adopting Sam and then our twins, aged four, Randi and I both figured our family was complete. With six kids, ages six and under, I began scheduling more parenting talks, mostly timed around the kids' bedtime, and Randi started falling asleep with the kids, sometimes earlier. She just wasn't the energetic night owl I had married.

Believe it or not, even with half a dozen little ones, the dust did start to settle after a couple of years. Call it a habit, an addiction, whatever, Randi and I agreed, "All right, one more. What's the difference—six or seven? A small percentage increase."

The dust—or maybe it was fog—kept clearing, and we kept thinking, "What's one more? It's chaos now," albeit a rich chaos. We enjoyed being Mom and Dad to a bunch, so we assumed we'd probably enjoy it more with a bigger bunch. Besides, you do improve. Randi once told me, "I think I'm a better mom of ten than I was of three." Either that or she's so brain-numbed that she doesn't even know the exact number anymore.

Many times I've seen parents experience the same chain of events Randi and I did. They may not adopt ten—everyone has his or her own personal load limit. But they discover, sometimes quite unexpectedly, that this kid thing could be more rewarding with a few more.

Why then did we stop at ten? Age—ours, not the kids'. God has reasons for limiting the child-bearing years. We figured we'd be wise to take a cue from his biological guidelines.

: : :

ANNUAL EVENT?

Dear Dr. Ray: For many couples, adopting only one child can take years. How did you and your wife adopt ten children in twelve years?

—*Really Curious*

Yours may be the most frequent personal adoption question I am asked. My answer would best begin with some thoughts on why in general adopting can take a long time.

Often I've asked teachers of parenting courses for pregnant high schoolers, "How many of your students consider placing their babies for adoption?" Answer: very few.

Now, given their young ages, the routine absence of a committed father and the extensive social and economic obstacles that an unwed mother faces, one would think this group likely to at least ponder adoption. That they seldom do is at the root of a numerical paradox in our society: While the number of pregnant single women has skyrocketed, the number of babies placed for adoption has plummeted. Recent figures have estimated around a million couples waiting to adopt and fifty thousand babies placed each year. The math tells the story.

The students' attitudes parallel the broader culture's. The majority of single mothers choose to keep their babies. A significant minority abort. Only a tiny fraction consider adoption. Why so few? The prevailing mind-set, particularly among younger mothers, is that raising one's child is the loving and responsible thing to do, however ill-prepared one might be for it.

Tragically, adoption is now more often viewed as a negative than as a positive. It is not seen as a sacrifice of love or a gift of two committed parents but rather as a sign of lack of love, lack of commitment. "I could never live with myself if I didn't keep my child." "How can you give away your baby?" "Won't you spend the rest of your life wondering about him or her?"

This attitude is reinforced relentlessly, not only by peers but by adults. "We'll do whatever you want" or "We'll take over however" are typical soon-to-be-grandparent reactions. Certainly the best of intentions and powerful emotions surround the decision to keep and raise a child. In recent years, though, the reluctance to even contemplate adoption, no matter what, has become the ascendant attitude.

Add to such thinking the fact that fertility problems among married people are rising—for reasons beyond the scope of this book—and you can construct the equation. More wishful parents plus fewer babies equals longer waits.

Most adoptive couples understandably are eager for a healthy, developmentally on target infant. They want to live the whole parenting journey from its beginning, giving to their child all the early social and emotional benefits of a good family. Indeed, given patience and perseverance, most do experience such an adoption, sometimes two. But if more than one or two children are a hope, in less time and with less expense, a core adoption reality comes into play: the more open a couple is to adopt a child who may not be "exactly" what they had initially anticipated —in gender, age, health, development, race—the more quickly the adoption will occur. To put the matter somewhat bluntly, the less in demand a child might be for others, the sooner he can become a part of your family.

Many things can make a child more available to be adopted— age, race, having a sibling or two also in need of a family, alcohol or drug exposure in the womb, developmental uncertainties, major or minor health issues. Am I saying that to adopt more kids more quickly you must look to a special needs population? Not always. But as a rule it does speed up the whole process.

Do some of our children have special needs? That depends upon whose definition you use. If you use my wife's and mine, no. If you use society's, yes. I'll elaborate in upcoming pages.

A closing thought: Ten kids in a little over twelve years involves a lot of factors coming together—prayer, timing, perseverance, searching, openness, blind luck and a willingness to adopt more than one child at a time. In the end everything funnels down to a simple fact: Many babies and children need a mommy and daddy, and if they are less than "perfect," they are really only like their parents-to-be.

chapter two

ADOPTION ADVICE WORTH IGNORING

Expert types have theories and advice about almost everything. Indeed, some experts think our society is "over-experted." Count me as one who thinks so, even as I write this book.

With all the opinions out there, how does one weigh them? How can one know what is accurate and what isn't, what will help and what will frustrate? Start by asking a few basic questions; at least, that's what I would advise.

Does the idea make sense? Just because someone with letters after his name proclaims something doesn't mean it's worthwhile or logical. The average person has a reservoir of reasoning with which to assess the soundness of a notion. Use yours. If something doesn't seem to make sense, it probably doesn't.

Does the idea square with reality? Again, most folks have a feel for the real. They can judge from experience what fits well with the world as they know it. A certain trustworthiness comes from common perception.

Does the idea sound way out? Experts are supposed to know more about their area of expertise than regular folks. Therefore, sometimes they can stretch hard for that novel insight, original observation or unique piece of guidance. But in the effort to demonstrate well-above-average understanding, sometimes they stretch too far.

What follows are notions put forth not by me but by other experts. You judge how much they should influence you. Don't just take my word for it.

∶ ∶ ∶

To the Rescue

Dear Dr. Ray: I read an article that said you should never adopt to "rescue" a child. Don't some kids need to be rescued?

—Moved to Move

Since I didn't read the article, I'm not sure what the author meant by *rescue*. Like so much communication, it's all in how you define your terms.

Certainly many adoptive parents have no intention of rescuing anyone. They want children and a family. In a way it is they who want to be rescued—from childlessness.

It's probably safe to say that the range of reasons to adopt is nearly as broad as the range of personalities of parents. Further, most people's motives are blended in with anticipation, hope, speculation, even reluctance. If rescue is somewhere in the mix, I'm not surprised.

Nevertheless, let's assume that the *main* motive to adopt is to rescue. That is, the child is desperately in need of a mom and dad, stability, security, affection, all of the above. And the parents want to provide what is needed. I'm perplexed over what could be wrong with that.

Maybe the objection is, "You shouldn't adopt out of pity." If one's foremost motivation is pity, minus much desire to be a parent, then I can agree that the initial impetus of pity will fade fast as the demands of being a good parent unfold month after month, year after year. In this limited sense, rescue as a reason won't pass the test of time.

For many, however, any urge to rescue is only one urge inter-acting with others. To advise that an adoption should be avoided if any part of it is colored by a saving mind-set, in my judgment is ludicrous.

The reality is that some kids do need to be rescued. They do need a much better environment to grow up in. What's more, it is often the children in the most deprived circumstances who most need to be pulled out of those circumstances. For a grown-up to recognize that, and be moved by it, is not a Don Quixote complex. It is awareness of a child's need and the willingness to act to meet that need.

Many who adopt do so from a morality grounded in religious beliefs. They are moved by their faith in God and a desire to live according to his principles. One of those core principles is to care for the most dependent and vulnerable. Most often that means children. Indeed, in the Bible are verses such as "Whoever receives one such child in my name receives me" (Mark 9:37) and "Religion that is pure and undefiled before God and the Father is this: to visit orphans and widows in their affliction..." (James 1:27).

If individuals adopt out of a sense of obedience to their deep-est convictions, is their decision somehow less psychologically healthy? Is the implication that they will be unable to sustain their commitment emotionally to the child once their initial "religious enthusiasm" recedes? What if the same religious enthusiasm fosters the drive to be not only a parent but an exceptional one? Couldn't one just as legitimately argue that other virtues of good parenthood—love, stability, patience, perseverance—would gain strength from the initial moral impetus to offer a child a home?

I guess we are back where we began. What does it mean to "rescue" a child? In all but the most extreme, narrow sense of the word, I do not see this motive as unhealthy, immature, unrealistic or self-focused. In fact, it would seem that it is active in many parents' desires to open their lives to a child.

If we label that a rescue, so be it.

: : :

REPLACEABLE PARTS?

Dear Dr. Ray: My husband and I were initially devastated by the medical diagnosis of our infertility. We have begun to look at adoption, but some have advised us not to adopt to "replace our lost children."

—*No Substitutes*

Infertility means different things to different people. But for most it means loss: the loss of parenthood as they envisioned it, the loss of biological offspring, the loss of the hopes, plans and goals they had for themselves and their family.

Some accept their infertility with resignation: "We can't conceive, so that's it. There will be no children in our future." Others look to adoption as a sort of "Plan B": "We can't have kids the natural and normal way, so we'll try to have them a secondary way." Still others see adoption as a viable, worthwhile road to a family, equal in all aspects to birth parenting except for the biological. And time confirms for them that the core connection to a child is not biology but love. They can't imagine loving their adopted child any more than they do.

Your reaction to your infertility has been compared by many in the adoption world to grief. While you didn't lose someone you actually knew, you did lose someone you mentally knew, however incompletely. Would she have your hair? What about personality? Would he be more like Mom or Dad or maybe Grandpa? Would your kids like the same sports and be as skilled at them as their dad? Would they be talkative and sociable from the start, like their outgoing mother? Images and expectations for offspring can fill one's mind.

Then comes the reality: Your birth child (or children) is not to be. The news is jarring, along with the altered self-image that can accompany it. A whole new family future has to be imagined, pondered. What was once accepted as a given—kids—now appears quite uncertain.

Fortunately, the human spirit is resilient. Most people with time adapt to their circumstances, consider their alternatives and move forward. They come to realize that children can be part of themselves in many ways, not only through genetics.

Replace seems like a pretty loaded word. It implies that the adopted child is a fallback, a fill-in, not completely wanted for himself but for a purpose—to provide a couple with a child-rearing experience.

In fact, the vast majority of adoptive parents-to-be don't see their adoptions in this light. True, they might struggle to work through their sense of loss over what might have been, but they don't regard adoption as an inferior answer to their loss. Indeed, most find their excitement building as they move closer to adoption.

I have a question for those who advise you not to adopt to replace your lost parenthood: At what emotional point should you adopt? Must you wait until you're psychologically certain that there is not the smallest of urges to replace? How about allowing yourself to adopt when replacing is a 50-percent factor? Twenty percent? Five percent?

If you're concerned about a "wrong" adoption motive, ask yourself, "Why do I want to adopt?" To pursue parenthood? To give a family to myself and to a child? To begin the journey to more children? All are healthy reasons. If they account for most or even much of your thinking toward adoption, you needn't be worried about some lingering or buried urge to find a birth child substitute. If it's there, it's likely minor. Further, it's almost certain to fade as you come to know and love your adopted child, one you'll quickly realize is no surrogate but a genuine, one-of-a-kind kid.

A wise man once observed, "I don't know if I've ever had a completely pure motive." He was not confessing that he was a conflicted or confused human being. Rather, he was acutely aware that the impulses underlying his behavior were routinely an amalgam of selfish and selfless, mature and immature, good and bad.

To at least some degree, it would seem that some adoptive parents are initially moved to relieve their sense of loss. After all, it was a major loss, an unexpected one. It's only natural to seek to restore balance. Motives and emotions are not static, however. They shift with time and life changes.

And there are few things more life-changing than the arrival of a child. Thoughts of what might have been will quickly yield to the reality of what is. A flesh-and-blood child is far more real than an image or hope from the past. He or she will indeed replace, in the healthiest sense, a mind's-eye picture.

∴ ∴ ∴

ADOPTION OVERDONE

Dear Dr. Ray: I read a book advising adoptive parents to talk often to their child about his or her special status. For example, we're supposed to regularly say to our son, "I'm so glad we adopted you." Or we should celebrate two birthdays, one for his birth and a second for his adoption day. It seemed a bit much to me.

—*Talking*

I'm familiar with such advice. I too have read it. I too think it gets carried away.

Much of such thinking is grounded in the self-esteem movement dominant in education and the social professions. That is, we must make absolutely certain a child knows how valuable, unique and special he is, through constant affirmation if necessary.

Sure, an adopted child is special to his or her parents. Sure, the adoption was hoped for, pursued, cherished. Sure, Mom and Dad are very pleased to have their son or daughter. But how much adoption talk is necessary or even beneficial? When does the well said become the over said? Why does a child need to be regularly reminded of the adoptive relationship? Isn't the plain old parent-child relationship the real foundation of everything?

A related rationale underlying adoption overtalk is that we need to counter any thinking in a child that somehow she is a second-class person—an adoptive Cinderella, if you will. Thus, emotionally reiterating how much we treasure her adoption day, how special adoption is, how unique she is and so on will go far to anticipate and we hope, eliminate any of her adoption angst, spoken or unspoken.

No doubt it is wise to share good adoption thoughts, more than a few times. However, does too much talking carry unintended effects? Will it prompt a child to question, "Who are you trying to convince, me or you?" Even for littler kids a natural tendency is to wonder, "Why are you so caught up in this?"

Adoption is special because it unites a child with parents and parents with a child. Of course, the relationship isn't biological. For that matter, neither is the husband-and-wife relationship. Most everything else in the day-to-day loving and raising of an adoptive child is the same as raising a birth child. Too much "You're so special because you're adopted" talk, to my ears, conveys to a child that he is more different than he really is. Rather than enhancing a view of oneself as a natural part of the family, it may lead the child to question it, particularly if there are biological siblings.

Almost all adoptees see their adoptive moms and dads as Mom and Dad, and they aren't excessively caught up in the details of how that all came about. The everyday realities of kidhood and family-hood occupy most of their thoughts. The level of adoption celebration some think necessary may in fact be much higher than what the kids want or need.

We expert types have a strong inclination to overanalyze. Indeed, my expert opinion is that much expert opinion looks too hard for psychological and emotional issues. Adoption overtalk seems a classic example of this tendency. Why would we need to continually reassure a child if we didn't think that he continually needed reassurance? What if a child is perfectly content with who he is? What if he doesn't think about adoption all that much? What if a boy's immediate, most pressing emotional questions are, "Can I have more cake? And can you fix the chain on my bike?"

Please don't mishear me. I am not saying that we should minimize a child's adoption concerns. I'm also not suggesting a "once said, enough said" attitude—though that's a good attitude for discipline. I am saying—for fear of repeating myself—that too much adoption talk may be as unwise as too little.

A good rule, one that comes up other places in this book, is to follow your child's lead. Talk adoption when you sense it's needed. Express positives if the situation seeks them. Don't keep revisiting the adoption for fear you could be missing something down deep in your child. Contrary to what we experts might think, often with kids nothing is down deep except what's showing on top.

You want to make your child feel special, really special? Make sure he knows every day, all the time, how much you love him because he is your son, not because he's your adopted son. That is the best way to make him feel very secure in who he is.

:   :   :

BIRTH DISORDER

Dear Dr. Ray: My spouse and I have three children, ages nine, seven and three. We're considering adopting, but people have advised us not to "displace" any of our kids in their birth order, especially our oldest.

—*Shifty*

If you do adopt, with four or more kids under age nine, the word *order* will take on a whole new meaning for you. Maintaining birth order could be the least of your worries. Maintaining daily order will be top priority.

First let's examine the whole birth order theory. It's gotten a lot of popular press. All manner of psychological ideas have been advanced about how a child sees himself because of his place in the family. One idea asserts that once a child's birth position is solidified, it shouldn't be moved, as that would force him or her to adjust to a new family role, with who knows what untoward effects.

My theory is that birth order theories have grown as families have shrunk. There are now far fewer oldest and youngest children and more older and younger ones. (Remember your grammar?) Not so many years ago, kids routinely shifted up and down the family order as a new baby was born, displacing the old baby, or as the oldest left home, effectively moving the second oldest into first place. Put another way, there was a lot more natural family shuffling with the coming and going of more children. That alone would make it harder for birth order notions to capture the cultural mind as they have in the past few generations.

Our first two children were Andrew and Hannah. Andrew was the older, Hannah the younger or the baby. Then Sarah came, pushing Hannah to the middle, with Sarah assuming the baby role. Two years later we adopted Sam. Hannah then became the upper middle child, Sarah the lower middle and Sam the new baby. A few more years and Jonathan and Joanna, both age four, arrived. Hannah now sat clearly near the top of the age pyramid, Sarah (age three) dropped two notches, and Jon and Jo became the new upper and lower middle children. Sam rested secure in the youngest position—but not for long.

The sibling relocations continued for several more years and kids. Only Andrew didn't budge in the birth order. Others were variously the baby, middle child, next to the youngest, oldest once removed, former upper middle and so on. By my calculations, over the years we've had four different middle children, leading me to question: How long does one have to be a middle child to contract "middle child syndrome"? While a child is smack in the middle, does he have acute middle child syndrome? Once the child leaves the middle, does he exhibit residual middle child syndrome? When we had only two children, with Hannah being the younger, did she suffer from latent middle child syndrome?

Some parents are convinced of the birth order effect because they see it firsthand in the personalities of the kids. I don't doubt their observations. But the better explanation is temperament. Kids are who they are by their inborn wiring, whether they're the first, last, only or middle child or second fraternal twin. It just happens that sometimes their innate personalities coincide with their "birth position personalities."

For example, a middle son may show some attention-seeking, impulsive behavior—a theorized quality of middle children "lost" between siblings. Most likely he still would do so were he the oldest or youngest. It's who he is. To confirm this, do a test. Adopt one or two kids, thus shifting the birth balance. Observe the dynamics. See if any personalities really change all that much. Go ahead, I dare you.

When scrutinized by the research, birth order is a really squishy concept. It doesn't appear to exert much of an impact on kids. It's a nice notion, it seems to have intuitive appeal, but it doesn't hold up well when critically examined.

Now on to possible effects of slotting a child into the family. Personally, my wife and I did not adopt older than our older children. The reason was not birth order but innocence. Often older adopted children, sadly, have had poorly protected young lives and thus are worldly for their age. Randi and I decided not to bring a child into our home who could introduce behavior and experiences that might tempt even our oldest children.

We did adopt two siblings who were older, and more unruly, than our two younger children. Being age four at the time, though, the twins didn't do much to influence Hannah, age five, and Andrew, age six. Did they bring some new behavior tactics to the two younger children? Sammy, age one, was oblivious, and for the most part, thirteen years later, he still is. Sarah, age three, did act up some to greet her new siblings, but it was nothing that couldn't be corrected with a little time.

My suggestion? Don't avoid adoption solely for fear of shifting the balance of sibling status.

Your three-year-old will likely adapt most quickly. Littler ones aren't all that complex in their feelings and reactions to change. The two older ones shouldn't be significantly jostled emotionally if the new sibling is younger. After all, in their eyes they still hold the top spots; you've just given them one more sibling to rule.

Where I would be cautious is in adopting a child older than all of your children. As noted, depending upon the child's history and circumstances, he could show your children a "maturity" from which you have so far shielded them. I'd never automatically advise against such an adoption. Some older kids, by nature or good nurture, are still kids at their age. Knowing all you can about a youngster's life should go far in guiding you to a smart decision for your family.

: : :

TOO OLD BY KINDERGARTEN

Dear Dr. Ray: Some theories say that personality is pretty much established by age five or six. What does that say about adopting kids older than that?

—*Older Than Six Myself*

Before pondering what any such theory might mean for adoption, let's ask the primary question: Is the theory true? If not, then whatever conclusions it leads to can be ignored.

The idea that personality is settled by the age of five or so has its roots back in the early years of psychology. It started with Freud, and others have since added their own twists to it. Research, experience and common sense have all shown it to be, at the least, incomplete or, at the most, wrong.

Yes, a child's innate personality, or temperament, is wired in young. It's genetically part of who he is. Also, many behaviors, traits and habits get a solid start in the first several years of life. To assert that personality is crystallized that young, however, or that it will stubbornly resist reshaping is quite a psychological stretch.

I don't know about you, but I'm very different now than I was at age five. My wife says I have the maturity level of a ten-year-old, which to me seems pretty high for a husband.

At age five or six, did you have any political party affiliation? Deep religious convictions? Moving on to second grade, what qualities did you value in a future spouse? Could you even read, much less know whether it's good strategy to call a draw play on third down and seven?

You don't need a rocket scientist's personality to know that who we are has virtually unlimited potential to change. For some more than others, change can be a slow, steep slog. Still the *potential* is there. Barring serious mental complications, it's there until life is over.

In almost everything we do, we are to some degree free to choose other than we always have or to act differently than we've acted in the past. In other words, we are not irresistibly bound to what we were but can recognize and work to alter whatever we wish about ourselves. Most folks, even we "shrink" types, would agree that if we grown-ups can change, kids are even more malleable.

Don't mishear me. (Is that part of your personality?) I'm not saying that a child's early life experiences don't matter. On the contrary, some kids experience neglect, trauma or misguided upbringing, and redirecting their personality, however young they are, can take a long time and great effort. Still, it is not impossible.

All else being equal, if a child has known turbulence at a young age, the sooner one removes the turbulence the better. All four children whom we adopted beyond infancy (ages two, three, four and four) had some nasty or chaotic experiences prior to coming to us. Nevertheless, ever so slowly over the years, what looked to be their personalities began to evolve. The kids gradually reflected more of our values, our expectations. To be sure, shyness essentially stayed shyness, impulsiveness continued as a lack of caution, and talkativeness morphed into verbosity. The essence of personality will remain somewhat durable; the expression of it can be influenced by parenting.

The children's personalities have come to reflect a complex interplay of their inborn wiring, early experiences and our family life. How it all will look with time only God fully knows. One thing is certain: We're feeling better with time about the direction.

To briefly reiterate (a personality trait I've had since the age of three):

1. Personality is *not* established by the age of six.
2. How a child's early life affects his later life depends upon many intervening factors, not the least of which is high-quality parenting.
3. Humans often change only by the inch, but the younger the human, the more quickly the inches come.
4. Some kids mature more from thirteen to sixteen than they do from five to thirteen.
5. If you wish to adopt an older child, realize that you will be loving and raising a unique personality from day one. *Unique* doesn't mean "set in stone."

: : :

Unfinished Business

Dear Dr. Ray: I've read articles stressing how much adopted children have a need to find birth parents, especially as they get older. My son is only six. So far he's shown no such desire. Is it coming?

—*Waiting*

Routinely I ask parents, adoptive and biological, "Based solely upon media messages and made-for-TV movies, what percentage of adoptive kids would you think seek out birth parents as young adults?" Answers? Anywhere from 50 to 90-plus percent, with most guesses toward the higher numbers. The perception has been solidified in the public's mind.

Some adoption professionals theorize nearly endlessly about the "unfinished business" and "need for closure" that emotionally follow a child into the adoptive world. Somewhere inside the child is wrestling with a sense of abandonment or a lack of wholeness or a nagging need to know more. Those conflicts percolate and can be suppressed only so long. Once adopted children are independent and able, they will seek. The psyche demands it.

That's the theory anyway. So what are the facts? The percentage of grown children who actually search for birth parents is under 10 percent. In other words, less than one in ten adopted children pursues the supposed universal need to know.

What if more than 10 percent want to know but don't act for a range of reasons—fear of hurting adoptive parents, uncertainty over who and what they might find, rejection from a birth parent, practical and legal hurdles, apathy? Certainly any of these, and more, could deter a search. But for how many?

Twenty percent? Fifty? Since we don't have data, we are in the realm of speculation.

Which pushes us back to theorizing, which pushes us back to guessing at the "true" numbers. Better to draw conclusions from what we do know. Only a tiny percentage of adoptees follow up on any impulse to seek, for whatever the reason.

Why such a discrepancy between the perception and the real? First of all, ours is an overanalyzing, over-psychologizing society. Sounds funny coming from a psychologist, doesn't it? Well, that's my analysis anyway. We probe intensely for internal upheaval, sometimes seeing it where little exists. In the over searching we even create it for some.

Second, certain kids, because of history or personality, do express more questions about their origins. Therefore the speculation follows that perhaps others have the same curiosity. They're just not as in touch with it or are reluctant to be forward about it out of feeling for their adoptive parents.

Third, people called experts in our society are afforded a certain credit or status by nonexperts. Thus, if the experts say such is so, that alone can make it so in the minds of some. Put another way, if a pro asserts that most adoptive kids have identity gaps that need to be filled, that must be the case. Experts know these things.

Perhaps the expert does know, but any theory about humans needs to be confirmed by evidence or at least by commonsense reality. So unless big numbers of young adult adoptees are silently struggling to resolve all manner of inner turmoil, it might be more accurate to conclude that for most, it's really not there.

My experience with adoption, professional and personal, confirms this. Almost all of the adoptees I've known consider their adoptive parents their parents. Further, the more loving the adoptee's family, the more warmly she also thinks of the birth parents, Mom in particular, even if not feeling a strong urge to connect, emotionally or geographically. Most kids derive their sense of self from a good family life. They simply don't report the "issues" that some theories propose they have. And I'm inclined to believe them.

In my own family, with five of our children between the ages of sixteen and twenty, one might think this is a peak time for questions about roots, especially given the general angst supposed to arrive naturally with adolescence. If so, the kids are keeping a lot of something from Randi and me. Certainly more curiosity could be coming, but so far the feelings expressed have taken mostly the tone of, "It's hard for me to imagine being anywhere else." My son once told his mother that the idea of any other childhood seemed unreal. He couldn't wrap his head around a world of other parents, other siblings, another family. This is the world he knows and the one where he is content.

Our five youngest pretty much live in the here and now, as do most little kids. For the most part the extent of their parental searching lies in looking for their mother when she tries to grab a few peaceful minutes in the bathroom. Of course, none of them drive, and neither can they cross the street without an adult, so their experience of world travel is fairly limited.

There is a phenomenon I call the "better parent fantasy." During edgy teen years or during conflicts over rules and limits, kids may express a wish for different parents. For the biological child this is a fantasy. He's stuck with these fossils whom he ranks near the bottom of preferred parental options until, that is, they yield to his wants. In the adoptive child's mind, that "better parent" could be out there somewhere. And life sure would be better with her or him. It couldn't be worse, especially when rated against the Neanderthals he's ended up with.

This attitude can mislead a parent into thinking a child has origin struggles when in fact he does not. The motive behind the adopted child's comments is most often passing frustration. "I want my real mom" statements don't typically emanate from unfinished psychological business. Rather they come from an "I wish I had an alternative to your parenting ways, and I might, you know."

An imperfect parallel can be drawn to the child of divorce who says, "I'm going to live with Dad (Mom)," when she doesn't like the rules of the resident parent. The child may think it the answer to the current distress, but it doesn't reflect an "I don't consider you my parent" sentiment. Most often, neither is that the true feeling of an adopted youngster.

To repeat for emphasis, nearly all adopted kids view their adoptive parents as Mom and Dad, not as substitutes or plan B or temporary stand-ins. They may love and respect the biological mom and dad they don't know, but the committed presence of the parents they do know gives them their identity and sense of wholeness. They feel little drive to seek, create closure or satisfy curiosity. They love how they are loved. And for them that is more than enough.

: : : chapter three : : :

ADOPTION SPECIAL EFFECTS

A scene in a popular animated superhero movie contains a classic line. Mother is driving her young son home from school. He is frustrated because she won't allow him to use his super racing abilities to compete against his classmates. In desperation he asks, "Why can't I just be a little special?"

Mom explains, echoing a modern self-esteem mantra, "Everyone is special."

To which he replies, "If everyone is special, no one is special."

Besides great racing talents, the kid has great insight. The broader a word's meaning, the less meaning the word has.

"Special needs" is a description well known in the adoption lexicon. And its meaning is expanding. As it does, more children are defined on paper as special, when in reality many of them might better be considered all too normal, in the most special sense of the word.

: : :

Too Much Specialness?

Dear Dr. Ray: What is "special needs" adoption? Do any of your children have special needs?

—*Need to Know*

Special needs is a broad term, and getting broader. It might be good to start by describing what a "special needs child" is not: The child is not a healthy infant of the same race as the adoptive parents.

Now let me tell you what a "special needs child" is: He may exhibit developmental, intellectual, psychological or social problems judged significant; she is sometimes part of an adoptable sibling group. In other words, age, race, health, history, birth family and womb environment can all make a child "special needs" by definition. Does that clear things up?

Twenty-five years ago I had no children and ten theories about parenting. Now I have ten children and no theories. Nonetheless, back then I wrote my first book, *You're a Better Parent Than You Think!* (Fireside, 1992). One of its chapters is titled, "Is My Child Normal?" It asserts that as more experts and "new and improved" notions permeate child rearing, the definition of *normal* is shrinking, so to speak. More behavior is becoming psychologically questionable.

To illustrate, a parent might ask me, "My child likes to play by herself. Is that normal?" Or, "My preschooler throws two or three fits a day. How typical is that?" Or, "My son is quiet. How do I know if he's too quiet?"

In the book I tagged the phenomenon "enlightened parent's disease." The main symptom is the wonder and worry that a child's behavior has meaning we're missing. Inundated by child-rearing theories and all the analyzing they encourage, we've grown psychologically vigilant, prone to overinterpret and over-label sometimes even the standard stuff of childhood.

Something similar is occurring in adoption. More kids are being tagged with "special needs" because they fall outside of a contracting range of "normal needs." Certainly there are kids who pose atypical challenges, for all kinds of reasons. The core question, however, is not, "Does this child exhibit special needs?" Again, by what and whose definition? The core question is, "How do these special needs translate into real-life child rearing?"

By conventional definition, nine of our ten children would be considered special needs kids, some in multiple areas. Seven are racially different from my wife and me. Four were adopted when they were older. Most were drug-exposed *in utero*, a few heavily so. Four were parts of sibling pairs. One came with a behavioral diagnosis. One was born with a physical problem needing several surgeries. Three were developmentally delayed.

All this looks like a clear special needs picture, doesn't it? Well, that depends upon what part of the picture one focuses on.

Seven of our children are above average to superior in intelligence. Of our five oldest, three began college early. While three of the kids do show some academic and learning delays, these are mild. There are no unmanageable behavior or psychological problems. A few of the kids are having more "growing pains" than their siblings, but that happens with any family of ten; it need not be due to special needs. Label it instead personality variability.

What about special race needs? I will talk more on that in a few pages (see "A House of a Different Color" in chapter four). For now let me pronounce: A kid is a kid is a kid. And skin color is meaningless in defining differences across kids. What about society's reaction? Again, that's a coming topic. For now I can state emphatically that neither we nor our children have experienced virtually any prejudice or negative reactions because of color.

In many if not most cases, *special needs* conjures up a specter of challenges and turbulence well beyond the eventual reality. For Randi and me the main impact of special needs has not been on our parenting. Rather it has been on the relative ease and speed with which we have been able to adopt. Had we been deterred by the "special needs" label, we would have lost out on knowing and loving many of our children.

Bottom line? We don't really consider any of our children to have notable special needs. They are children, widely diverse in their personalities, abilities, weaknesses and approaches to life. Indeed, aren't we all?

Perhaps the best thought on this subject comes from the children's mother. Someone once asked Randi, "Aren't you afraid of what problems the kids could confront you with, especially as they get older?" Her answer, "If the kids have problems, they'd probably have them with us or without us. I'd rather have them be with us."

:   :   :

The Special Needs List

Dear Dr. Ray: My wife and I are considering adopting a child with special needs. The agency gave us a long list of medical, developmental and behavioral needs, and we are to identify which we would and would not consider. We feel as if we're picking who to accept and who to reject. We wouldn't have that option if the child were born to us.

—*Torn, Many Times*

My wife and I had a similar reaction during a couple of our adoption screenings. We too pondered such lists and had to note which kids were "OK" for us and which weren't. The process evoked an uneasy sense of pickiness, almost like mail ordering a child from a catalogue. After all, we weren't open to everything, just some things. What's more, considering each need one by one reinforced the idea that perhaps we weren't as open as we had thought.

The choices can be heavy. While a child with a serious illness might be considered, what about a terminally ill child? Missing fingers or wheelchair-bound? Early neglect versus a history of sexual abuse? Mild learning problems or an IQ below 50? Attention deficit hyperactivity disorder or autism? A child whose birth parent had serious mental illness? A three-year-old with emotional troubles? A twelve-year-old with emotional troubles?

The scope of needs encompasses those barely atypical to the traumatic, from negligible impact on family life to intense. How does one draw the line separating the very doable from the limits of one's ability?

Fortunately, initial emotional reactions often dissipate in the face of reason and more information. As Randi and I pondered the list and ourselves, we came to better understand why the process is necessary—more than that, why it is good.

First are the hard facts. There are kids with all manner of needs and handicaps. Some are extremely difficult to place. Fortunately, there are parents willing to provide homes across the need spectrum. The task of an agency is to begin the matching process for parent and child. How else but to ask who would be open to what?

Second, because *special needs* is so broad, saying one is open to special needs is likewise broad. It is something that has to be clearly and individually defined. Specifically, what does each parent mean by *special needs*? The list is a concrete way to put some particulars on general desires.

Third, many folks, upon seeing up close the full diversity of kids, open wider their hearts and homes. They are moved by all the children who, while not "perfect" physically or otherwise, in all other ways are still kids who share one main need—the need for a mom and dad.

Fourth, weighing all the needs may initially make some ask, "How open am I really?" That question, though, is best answered in a broader context. What are parents able to handle given their own state of life? Are there other children in the home? What demands already exist? What are the careers and work schedules of the parents? Finances? Social and family supports? Personalities and emotional makeups? These factors and more all interact to answer the question of which special needs are most likely to be successfully integrated into the home.

Then again, no decision has to be made solely from paper. Behind each description stands a flesh-and-blood child, with all the fullness of kidhood wrapped around his particular needs. Therefore any condition can be marked "to consider," but the ultimate question of whether or not to adopt will depend upon having more information.

Further, many children have more than one special need. A child with a cleft lip and palate may be of a different race than you, have been exposed to drugs in the womb and show some mild developmental delays. The list attempts to narrow down what needs or combination of needs you would consider yourself able to adopt.

I remember mulling over our possibilities with Randi when we already had several children under age eight. The workload wasn't all that heavy for me: I pretty much hid in the den and wrote parenting books. Randi, though, who shouldered the heavy lifting of family life, every few days did need some sleep.

Seriously, what was already on our plate weighed heavily in choosing what more to add. In the end we realized we would do better with some special needs and not others, as each was judged in light of our family life and personal limits.

Did we feel heartless, less noble, because we bypassed some children? A little, at first. Still, good decisions have to be a blend of head and heart, at least that's what our head said. We had to assess what we could realistically assimilate into our family.

Not uncommonly spouses have varying ideas about what they can assimilate as parents. You and your wife may be open to very different levels of need. A general suggestion for resolution: The spouse who does more of the everyday parenting has the greater voice. In our situation I deferred to Randi's judgment on any condition about which we weren't of one mind, as much of the day-to-day family operation is hers. In other families with other structures, the parents must work through—if necessary, compromise on—what is acceptable to both.

In the end, accepting any degree of special needs has to be agreeable, even if unequally, to both parents. Put another way, each spouse has veto power, as a commitment to a child—special needs or no—has to be shared, though the initial level of enthusiasm might not be shared. While one spouse might be moved deeply to reach far into the needs continuum, without the other spouse's being at least somewhat nearby in willingness, the adoption could be a source of discord from the start. Children with significant special needs pose demands enough without being raised in the context of parental conflict over those needs.

You observed, "We wouldn't have the option to accept or reject a child born to us." True. But there is an element of discretion present in an adoption that isn't present in a natural birth. Pregnancy most often leads to a baby, who one hopes is healthy. If not, we accept and reshape our lives to care for our little one who is now here. Adoption, especially of older children or infants with atypical needs, grants some latitude to deliberate one's course of parenthood. With your adoption you are choosing some degree of challenge. That's a very open attitude, I think.

Ponder the list with your wife. Recognize that some problems will be an "easy" acceptance; others will unnerve you; most will be somewhere in the "need more information" group. Instead of feeling bad about whom you aren't considering, feel good in knowing whom you will consider. And always remember, all children have one overarching need—the need for a parent.

:   :   :

A SPECIAL PARENT

Dear Dr. Ray: You are a psychologist. You are trained to deal with problems. Would the typical parent be as able as you to raise special needs children?

—*Average Mom*

I am a psychologist, but please don't hold that against me. I think I have as much common sense as the next parent.

Because of my degree or my experience, some may believe that I am better equipped to raise children who pose some challenges. (Doesn't raising any child pose some challenges?) My answer to that? Well, yes and no. You see, I even talk like a shrink. Call it my training.

Yes, being a psychologist may give me an advantage. But it's not the advantage most folks think. My advantage is that after years—decades, actually—of working with parents and kids, my sense of what kids are like has sharpened. Whatever special needs are present or could arise as our children grow, they won't confuse or distress me as much as they otherwise might have.

Put another way, I'm not as shaken over the jerks and quirks that can come with kids of all stripes—special needs or not. Consequently, I may be able to ride the child-rearing waves a little more steadily and react with a little less second-guessing than others.

Granted, that is a real plus in parenting. It is not, however, the benefit most people conjure up when thinking "psychologist."

Which brings me to the "no" part of my answer. No, being a psychologist does not greatly elevate my parenting, if by *psychologist* one means "a person having technical knowledge." In other words, as a professional do I possess tools, methods and sticker-system savvy well beyond that of everyday mortals to guide the most recalcitrant youngster to full psychological well-being? Alas, I wish it were so.

Being a good parent is grounded in some basics—love, morals, confident authority, supervision, common sense and good judgment. None of these are tied to special techniques or professional wherewithal. They are the quintessential stuff of motherhood and fatherhood. They make one more able to raise any child. Indeed, I've known quite a few "amateurs" who are far more effective and successful parents than some of the most credentialed and psychologically enlightened mental-health types.

My advice as a trained professional? Never be limited by your lack of "up-to-date" child-rearing know-how. The qualities most crucial to being a good mom or a good dad abide within you and not within books. Of course, learning and experience improve the best of parents. But being a strong, competent parent begins not with a degree in psychology, social work or child development; it begins inside you. It begins with the person you are. It always will.

: : :

NOT READY TO BE CANONIZED

Dear Dr. Ray: We have three adopted children, two with some special needs. Both my husband and I are embarrassed by other's comments about how special we are—even that we're "saints." Our kids are still young (under age eight), and I don't want them hearing this as they get older.

—*No Saint*

You don't have to read between my lines to deduce that I think adoption is a beautiful thing. It lets big people be loving parents, and it lets little people have loving parents. Much of the time it's not easy to figure out who benefits the most.

People's reasons for adopting, of course, vary. Some want children and a family life. Some want to give a home to a child who, because of life's circumstances, may not so easily find one. Others find themselves, maybe unexpectedly, in a position to pick up the pieces in a child's existence. Some marry the child's mother or father.

To the degree that others see you as motivated beyond the "typical"—the desire for a child—they are likely to see you as doing something special, even heroic, more so if they acknowledge they couldn't or wouldn't do it. You adopted three children, two of whom require extra parenting. Truth of Life number 103 states: The higher someone reaches to do something I'm not doing—for whatever the reason—the higher my regard for that person.

Someone's imparting to you noble impulses is embarrassing, perhaps because, in your mind, that perception may not be accurate. While you're parenting with more effort now, you didn't necessarily plan to do that. You simply wanted kids and a family. How they came and who they were was secondary.

Then again, maybe you did seek harder-to-place children. Healthy babies are quickly adopted, and you looked for kids who weren't in the highest demand. It's understandable, then, why some folks admire you. They value anyone who gives of the self—every day—to another.

Want to deflate your status fast? Try, "I really don't appreciate your calling me a saint, and the next time you do, I'm going to punch you in the head." "Maybe I am a saint, but anyone would be if they had to live with (insert spouse's name here)." "My kids don't always think I'm so sweet. Sometimes they think I'm the wicked witch of the East."

If you're not quick on your verbal feet—a common result of living with three kids—you still can redirect "undeserved" compliments. With a sweet or, if you will, "saintly" smile, you might acknowledge, "We're grateful to have our little family." Or, "We didn't think we were going to have children, so this is an unexpected blessing." Or, "We prayed to have a family, and God gave us one."

You're not trying to convey, "I'm such a saint that I even respond with obvious humility to anyone noticing how saintly I am." No, you're honestly putting the truth out front: "We're getting a lot more than we're giving."

Time will help solve your dilemma. Many, if not most, accolades come from those only superficially familiar with your family. Your relatives and close friends probably don't repeatedly pat you on the parenting back. They know you know what they think, so they don't reiterate it every time they hear one of your kids say, "Please," unprompted or, "Excuse me," after burping the alphabet. With those closest to you, any expressed awe over your super parenting status cools eventually. In fact, every few months you might want to confirm that they're still thinking it. "So do you still think I'm a saint? Just checking."

It's easier for you, the adult, to let the "Are you related to Mother Teresa?" compliments pass. You can put them in perspective. Such praise is more ticklish when made within kid earshot. The message sent, however unwittingly, can be, "How wonderful of you to take in these children, whom many others wouldn't want."

To be charitable, most of the time this isn't another's meaning. Nevertheless, it can be what a child hears. Therefore, I recommend once again that you gently deflect the remarks. You won't just nudge the attention off you; you will let both the adult and your kids hear how much you appreciate your family.

What if someone lingers on the saintly theme despite your best efforts to change the subject? Take her aside privately. Point out softly that you'd never want any of your kids to think you did some kind of noble deed for an adoption cast-off. Most people would be surprised to hear that the kids could mishear their good words. Still, most would be sensitive enough to recognize the possibility. And for the sake of everybody, they'll cease.

So do I personally think you're a saint? That depends. How tough are your kids, and how much whining are you doing about them? Are you carrying 87 percent of the load, as my wife does? I do write about child rearing, however, mostly while she's doing laundry, sweeping, schooling, bathing, transporting, soothing, separating, counseling. Sometimes I'll ask her to keep it down, especially if I'm trying to finish a paragraph on self-sacrifice.

In the end, whether your parenthood is as saintly as others think is God's call. Something tells me you know that. Know also that your kids aren't looking to be raised by a saint, though it would help. To live with a run-of-the-mill, loving mom is what they want. It's the crucial first step in helping *them* grow in character and perhaps, into sainthood.

chapter four

ASSORTED ADOPTION ANXIETIES

The number of people wanting and willing to adopt would be higher except for one thing—they're scared. An adoption colleague of mine calls it "the fear factor." It's fueled by a group of worries and *what-ifs?* that have the potential to squash any serious thought of adopting.

Psychologists advise that one way to reduce the controlling power of fears is to challenge them rationally. In other words, what is the *real* likelihood they will happen? What is the actual probability something will adversely affect our lives?

Surveys have shown that most people fear more those risks less likely to befall them—shark bites, terrorists attacks, air crashes, abductions—than those more so. I won't identify those here for fear of raising your anxiety.

So too in adoption—the anxieties that keep some from adopting are, thankfully, far less real than the media, the conventional wisdom (an oxymoron) and popular notions present. Let's rationally confront some common worries much less likely to occur than is pervasively believed.

: : :

The Genetic Objection

Dear Dr. Ray: What can we say to those who warn us, "Aren't you nervous about the genetic makeup of an adoptee? After all, you really can't know."

—*Unknown*

A simple rule of life: You don't have to answer every question. Actually, you don't even have to know the answer to every question. I'm a psychologist, one who lives in the realm of questions. Sometimes I just shrug my shoulders, smile a little and answer, "Good question."

Since you're probably not a psychologist, you may feel more pressure to give an answer to something asked of you just because it was asked. So I'll try to help. Good question.

First of all, no parent, biological or adoptive, can fully know what genetic makeup will be expressed in a child. The offspring of two parents is a unique individual, genetically unlike either Mom or Dad. Indeed, it is impossible to gauge—except in certain clear-cut genetic disorders—which genes will interact with which other genes to create the child. Mom and Dad may "know" the gene pool from which God formed their child, but they can't know the unfathomable combinations all interplaying to make up this absolutely one-of-a-kind human.

Furthermore, even though ambitious attempts to "map" the human genetic code have been proceeding for some years, this knowledge has not trickled down to the everyday understanding of the vast majority of people. Meaning, when someone asserts, "You can't know what you're getting," he is really saying, "No one can know because it's just not possible yet, if ever." Human genetic understanding is revealing one overarching reality: The more we know, the more we realize there is to know.

Now you may be saying, "Hold on, Dr. Ray—in some abstract sense your argument may be true, but most people are not looking from this logical angle. They simply mean that a lot less is known about the genetic history of an adoptive child than that of a biological one. And lurking in that history could be some innate trouble that no one can know is coming until it shows itself."

True, but again, to a degree this is true with any child. One can't fathom what inborn predispositions are present and how they may be expressed years later. This is an unchallengeable reality of our existence.

For debate's sake, however, let's allow the questioner to set the terms of the question. That is, let's acknowledge that, kid for kid, there may be more uncertainty in the "wiring" of an adoptive child than a biological one.

To address this, adoption professionals routinely explore the biological family history to provide a good medical picture for prospective adoptive parents. If there are potential genetic conditions, physical or mental, every effort is made to identify them. The adoptive child is not a blank genetic slate allowing only speculation of what might be hidden. In many if not most cases, "You don't know what you're getting" is inaccurate. You know more than one might think.

The most convincing answer to the genetics objection is still left. Assume little or nothing genetically is known. Assume the medical history is an empty record. Assume you suspect that the family history is suspect. A marvelous and consoling truth of our creation is that, for most of our existence, genetics is not destiny.

Yes, our genes, alone or in combination, do lead to particular dispositions, good or bad, helpful or harmful, for all of us.

Nevertheless, the full composition of who we are is an unfathomably complex interplay of genes and environment, or as the shrinks say, nature and nurture. If a child has a genetic leaning toward learning problems or asthma or impulsiveness, a mom and dad (nurture) are still influencing and shaping in response to that child's unique makeup (nature).

My children are wildly diverse in their development, intellect, temperament and almost every other aspect of personhood. Of course, most parents of a bunch of kids, birth or adopted, can observe a similar diversity. Indeed, the more kids you have, the more obvious will be the innate differences, even if all flower from the same two plants.

Despite my kids' genetic differences, all are being raised with sameness in expectations, morals and discipline. We hope this consistency will lead to similarity in character down the road. Genetics may be the foundation of the road, but Mom and Dad are driving the bus. The kids sit in separate seats, but the bus is going in the same direction.

Once more, "you can't know what you're getting." Absolutely true, no one can, be it with a birth or an adopted child. Much of the genetic world lies beyond our control, even understanding. Yes, there may be more unknowns in the histories of adoptive children, but how and where those unknowns become known is the big unknown. If one wants certainty in life, having a child is not the place to start.

Last and most critically, whatever one's genetics, in most expressions, they are powerfully affected by one's experiences. I think it's safe to say that most adoptive parents are genetically inclined to shape and influence their kids in the most positive direction possible.

CRACKED UP?

Dear Dr. Ray: Some years ago the media talked a lot about "crack babies"—children exposed in the womb to cocaine— and all the developmental problems that would cause. As a prospective adoptive mom, I'll admit this still scares me.

—*Hyper*

The media talk a lot about a lot of things. That doesn't mean they're accurate. I too recall the "crack babies" hysteria. The picture presented went something along these lines: Given the epidemic of drug abuse, particularly stimulants, among pregnant mothers, the neurological makeup of their babies in the womb would be dramatically compromised. The results would be children who are "hyper," have learning struggles and display attention and focus deficits. Perhaps most ominously, such children would be challenges to socialize, as they would be slow to develop self-control, even consciences.

There is only one problem with this picture: It is questionable at best, inaccurate at worst. Yes, one study did conclude that cocaine exposure negatively affects the developing baby, but several others did not find any such relationship.

Am I saying that drugs in a mother are of no consequence for a child? Absolutely not. Obviously, the healthier the womb, the better for the child. Just because a baby might survive in a womb that is a bath of chemicals doesn't mean the bath is good for him or her. What I am saying is that the "crack baby" scare was, pardon the phrase, a bit of hype, especially in its long-term, worst-case-scenario predictions.

What do studies actually find? Well, there is good news and bad news. The good news? Babies in the womb show surprising resistance, resilience even, in response to many toxins. The bad news? Prolonged unhealthy womb surroundings certainly can impact a child's development—sometimes obviously, more often in subtle ways.

The crack scare arose in part from attempts to link a particular drug to one particular set of complications. This is a daunting task. Not only is crack cocaine often one drug among several abused, but the abuse almost always occurs alongside other risk factors: poor prenatal care, inadequate nutrition, cigarette-smoking, high maternal stress, prematurity, low birth weight. It is this complex mix of negatives that *can* lead to problems in infancy and later. The child could have some learning troubles or could display a difficult personality. Or some developmental or social immaturity could be present. These are all possibilities, but not necessarily probabilities. Some professionals, me included, would argue that they're not even the standard outcomes—good health is.

One notable exception to all these perplexing pieces of the puzzle is alcohol. Plenty of research attests to its potentially devastating and fairly well-described effects on the developing baby, especially when alcohol is abused early in pregnancy. Then again, not uncommonly, alcohol is misused along with drugs.

However ugly the prenatal environment, the long-term picture still depends upon the interaction of many other factors: When in the pregnancy was the abuse and how long, the genetic strength of the baby, the genetic makeup of the birth mom, the quality of medical care, the overall health of the baby and the mother. It is nearly impossible in most cases to say, "This will lead to that." Which is what the cocaine hypothesis attempted to do, and which is why it eventually lost traction.

Nevertheless, just the possibility of developmental harm is enough to birth second thoughts about adoption for many, even changing some minds altogether. Indeed, we adopted more than once after other prospective parents became nervous over the kids' histories and withdrew their interest. That was many years ago; how are the children doing now?

I'm proud to say that their probation officer claims they are some of the nicest kids he has...just being silly! He really didn't say that. Seriously, other than some immaturity and learning troubles in a few, they sure look like typical kids to me.

The sad fact is that some children don't live in the healthiest wombs—drug-exposed or not. Despite that, many still grow up normally. What's more, good, solid parenting can go far in smoothing developmental bumps rooted in the earliest days of life. To be sure, some womb-challenged kids become child-rearing challenges. They will need better parenting than most. The fortunate fact is that most parents are capable of better parenting if their child needs it.

:   :   :

A House of a Different Color

Dear Dr. Ray: My race is Caucasian. I'm very open to adopting biracial or African-American children, but I'm worried about cultural issues and others' acceptance of the children and my family.

—*Mixed Feelings*

Some years ago I was listening to a sociologist on an afternoon talk show. The topic was the adjustment—present and future—of African-American children adopted by white parents. She had extensively researched the question. Her conclusion? Kids adopted cross racially into loving families do quite well as adults, notably in the area of race relations. Contrary to popular misperception, they are not racially adrift but are actually more settled than most in their feelings and acceptance of race.

Adoption professionals acknowledge that placing a minority child is more difficult than Caucasian placement. While there are more than enough white homes available for white infants, there are currently more adoptable African-American infants than African-American homes waiting to adopt. All else being equal, a child would be better adopted by parents of his own race, for a host of social reasons. However, if the number of adoptees exceeds the number of same-race adopters, then for the child's sake, other races need to be considered.

Even as more parents are willing to adopt cross racially, anxieties similar to yours restrain many. A foremost concern is, "What about culture? How do I keep the child's native culture alive?"

I must admit, I'm more than a little perplexed by this line of questions. First of all, what is "culture"? How is it defined, particularly in a child's life? Is it his or her past environment? Early life? What if neither was stable? Would one want to keep alive any aspects that might not be good or healthy for the child? If culture is considered a shared set of morals, ideas and philosophy of life, certainly the adoptive parents become the main influence and source of culture.

Is culture racial identity? Again, I'm not sure what that all entails. Many of my friends—and family—are of other races. We socialize together, attend the same churches and activities, live in the same neighborhood, shop at the same stores, play sports together—in essence, we pretty much live alike. Is it accurate to say that much, if not most, of our respective cultural identities are similar? Yes, there are differences in certain preferences and expressions of family life, but overall we are far more similar than not.

What about the family bond? Are my children my children, or not quite completely? Is James, my African-American son, who has been with us since age three, somehow less "complete" as a person because he is raised in my home with my values and outlook? Does this rob him of something? And if so, what?

On a radio talk show, one adoption "expert," adamantly opposed to my adopting minority children, cited as cultural hurdles, believe it or not, skin and hair care. I don't know if she was pleased with the eloquence of my answer, but basically I said, "A kid is a kid is a kid." James is my son, and neither skin nor hair has any meaning in defining some sort of racial identity gap between us. If I were to elevate physical features to prime status in cultural identification, then I look more like James than I do any of my daughters. My wife says I look most like Max. He is a cute dog.

After a parenting seminar a woman asked, "What will you do if one of your African-American sons at age fourteen says, 'I don't have to listen to you. You're not my father. You're not even my race!'" My sensitive psychologist answer? "You mean before I give him a stupid look or after?"

All my children are equally my children, whatever their roots. From the very beginning of our adoptions we never questioned that truth. Therefore, if any of the kids ever state, "You're not my real mom"—or dad, or race, or any other variant—we set the record straight immediately. Then we can talk about whatever prompted the remark.

Are we being insensitive to the children's feelings? I don't believe so. It is a statement of unalterable fact: You are my child—always and in all ways. Nothing can make that less true, least of all your appearance.

Being a colorful family has had its moments. When the children were younger, and the whole gang would trek with my wife and me to the grocery store, we shared some good giggles over people's perplexed stares, their pondering glances and—my favorite—the counting. We have three white, two Hispanic, two biracial and three African-American children. Every so often somebody who couldn't control his curiosity would ask, "Is this some kind of club or something?" Or people would look at Randi and me, and we could read their eyes: "I wonder if they know how this all happened?"

To others looking from the outside, we might appear to be a unique sort of family. Looking from the inside, all we see are our children, who are like all children. They misbehave, play, bicker, laugh, weasel, hug, resist rules—you get the picture.

As I get older I find that if I pay attention, life will correct me. Several kids over it's shown me that whatever race or culture "issues" (as I "shrink" more, I like that word less) our children could face, there need never have been a fear of or obstacle to my becoming their father. What's more, my family life has taught me firsthand that people are much more colorblind than popular media would have us believe.

My wife and I wanted children. The children needed a family. Those were the "right now" realities. The *what-ifs?* of culture and race may or may not ever happen. The today rewards of a son or daughter dwarf the someday possibility of cultural or racial question marks. To paraphrase the cliché, love conquers much. And much love conquers even more.

On a closing personal note, Randi says that Max and I do share similarities in skin and hair. He's getting those moles on his face too, and he's shedding a lot lately.

:   :   :

FOREVER DIAGNOSED?

Dear Dr. Ray: We have the opportunity to adopt a little boy and girl, siblings, ages six and three. The brother has been diagnosed with oppositional defiant disorder. We're a little nervous about what we might be dealing with.

—*Not a Therapist*

Some pages ago we interpreted the term *special needs*. The main point was that a lot of what is called "special needs" doesn't complicate the child-rearing journey as much as one might expect. In other words, "special needs" is often more special by definition than by daily life.

That resaid, behavior diagnoses are not uncommon among older adoptees. Many have had tumultuous early childhoods. Their family life was fragmented, neglectful or abusive, lasting sometimes several years before coming to the attention of protective agencies, who then took custody of the kids.

When parenting is poor, it's poor in manifold ways. Not only are love and stability lacking or missing, but so too are supervision, discipline, consistency—in essence, the keys to socializing and moralizing a child.

If a youngster isn't given what he needs in order to learn how to get along in the world, that kid can look pretty "disordered." Behavior can be erratic, immature, unpredictable—that is, oppositional and defiant. Through mental health assessment such kids may receive a behavior diagnosis, most frequently oppositional defiant disorder or conduct disorder. Both reflect that the child's behavior is a poor fit—no pun intended—with authority and social norms.

To be sure, some kids by nature are more inclined than others to resist rules and authority. They are wired to be more rebellious. On the other hand, some children would be beautifully well adjusted if raised in a healthy home, but because they lived, even for a few years, in a disordered setting, their learning, not their nature, was primary in forming and fueling their difficult conduct. And it is such conduct that can lead to a diagnosis.

Which leads to the question, how much will the behavior improve if the environment does? Can a good family turn around a lot of bad history?

Of course it can. Not necessarily quickly or smoothly, but the die—or if you will, the diagnosis—hasn't been irreversibly cast. Can you know for sure who will heal from a hurtful home life if given a healthy one? No. But a loving, strong parent can do much to put a child on the path to recovery.

Two of our children were adopted at age four. Their first fifteen months, from what we know, were quite erratic. The kids were shuttled from place to place; neglect was likely present, and chaos permeated their little lives. Although we weren't privy to exactly how much chaos, we know that it was enough to get the children removed from their birth parents and placed in foster care.

The foster parents were caring people but exerted little authority. The children had affection with few limits, love with little discipline. This was the pattern for nearly three years. Consequently, when we began our preliminary adoption visits, the kids we met were a tad rambunctious, to put it delicately. During those first few contacts, so to speak, my son smacked me in the face, attempted to strangle my wife and threw some fiery fits. Having adopted four infants prior, this was our first up-close adoption experience with undisciplined older kids. It wasn't pretty.

The agency scheduled an evaluation with a local psychologist to assess my son's, how shall we say, lack of impulse control and "anger management issues," from which he did get a couple of preliminary diagnoses, one being—surprise—a behavioral one. I was still reserving judgment. Sure, my son was pretty unpleasant, but given his history, both as an infant and preschooler, what could we expect?

Fast forward to now, thirteen years later. The diagnoses have faded. It appears that the lack of good, strong guidance those first four years had covered the children's inborn personalities. Now both have emerged as personable, even a bit low-key. They are seniors in high school. There have been no legal problems, no alcohol or drug use, no major social challenges. The kids are moral, pleasant young adults moving well toward independence. Despite some questionable early chapters, the book is now reading positively.

Reverse the parenting direction, and one can begin to reverse the behavior direction. It's a little more work than one might expect in parenting. But being a good parent is work.

Now to the $64,000 question: How long did it take us to turn around most of the early behavior trouble? The answer is mixed. The defiance abated fairly quickly, in less than a year. The kids didn't take long to realize that their mommy and daddy would respond quite differently to the very same habits that once succeeded in making other adults yield. As that awareness sank in, the behavior blasts became fewer and farther between.

All was not uniformly rosy, of course. Woven throughout the kids' learned opposition were some social immaturity and slight developmental delays. It was these characteristics that more slowly faded over the years. In other words, the oppositional defiance went away; the impulsive immaturity hung around awhile.

So am I telling you to ignore any behavior diagnoses? Am I saying that they are just leftover descriptions of an old life that will fade with a new life? Nope. Some diagnosed kids will definitely be tougher to raise. But the diagnosis is not necessarily indelible.

While you have no guarantees that the child will outgrow the label in his years with you, the chances are fairly good. I'd say they are more in your favor than not, and this makes them more in the child's favor too.

:   :   :

STUDY HARD

Dear Dr. Ray: Our agency requires an evaluation of us as part of its adoption process. We understand it to be a rather extensive series of interviews to determine how "fit" we are to adopt. Talk about making me nervous. Any calming words?

—*Fit Enough?*

You could do what my wife was tempted to do as we faced our first such interviews. She asked the adoption worker if she could use a stand-in for me, just for the early meetings. She told me not to take it personally.

OK, she really didn't do that. She was perfectly willing to have me analyzed, as long as I didn't talk.

A home study, as it is commonly called, is a requirement for almost all adoptions. Typically it is conducted early in the adoption process, as parents begin to work through an attorney or agency. You're right—it is a series of interviews and meetings conducted by a qualified professional, usually a social worker. The particular questions asked vary somewhat by evaluator. Overall though, the intent is to take a close look at the prospective adoptive parents—their marriage, home life, emotional makeup, religious views, motivation to adopt, child-rearing attitudes, other children if present, extended family relations and support, hobbies, interests, life goals. In other words, it is to gather relevant information to help assess people's suitability to be parents, for the first time or again.

Described this way, it can sound a little intimidating, can't it? Indeed, aren't you—how you think and live—being scrutinized? What if you don't measure up? What if you get an assessor who doesn't personally relate to you or approve of something about you? How do you know what that assessor is looking for? What if your answers are "incorrect"? What if you're solid but your spouse is questionable (my wife's concern)?

If you wonder what your personal nooks and crannies are hiding that might be an obstacle to your adopting, you could make yourself really nervous. But take it from one who assesses people for a living and who has personally been through several home studies—the reality is nowhere near as unsettling or emotionally risky as the anticipation. In fact, after the first few studies, I did so well that my wife invited me to the later ones. She actually gave me the correct time and place of the meetings.

Yes, you will be asked about personal, sometimes private matters. And you may feel anxious over exactly how to answer, because in your mind much is at stake. After all, you're not talking about buying a new car. The questions, however, are not designed to trap you or to build an escalating series of tests for making the adoption grade.

Primarily the purpose is twofold: One, to put together an accurate picture of who you are, as individuals and as a family and two, to serve as a general screening tool for uncovering any areas in your lives that could impact your suitability as adoptive parents.

Obviously, if your spouse has an ongoing alcohol problem, or you are facing serious financial struggles, or one of your children has a history of violent, explosive conduct, or you have neared divorce in the past, these are weighty matters that can affect whether an agency or attorney will recommend you as a prospective adoptive family. The reality is, however, that most folks pass through a home study relatively unscathed. I might even say "breeze" through it.

First of all, those who want to adopt are a pretty stable bunch. They are seeking a son or a daughter, and they are at least minimally aware that their lives have to be in reasonable order to successfully enter the adoption arena. They recognize that they won't get too far in the process otherwise.

Second, the home study is not designed to eliminate prospective parents. As I've said, it is designed to flag any potentially serious problem areas. Your sports enthusiasm versus your spouse's sports apathy, or your disparate bedtimes, or your introversion compared to your spouse's extroversion or, heaven forbid, the fact that you're a Yankee fan while your spouse is a die-hard

Red Sox rooter are not revelations of consequence. They are well within the normal variety of personalities and preferences.

The home study is not a rigid template within which you must fit in order to pass on to the next adoption phase. To be sure, examiners vary in their approaches and attitudes. They are people too—honest—with their personal ideas about what makes for a healthy family life.

In one of our early home studies, we were asked if we had separate bedrooms for each child in our family. Since we had two kids at the time, we did. But a room for another? I said, "We can add on if necessary."

Can you imagine that question now? Our house would need eleven bedrooms. Most certainly I wouldn't be writing this book; I'd be too exhausted from working four jobs. But no other adoption worker has since asked about bedroom numbers versus kid numbers.

Another trick question came up in our first home study. The social worker naturally asked about our marriage. I, the easygoing, do-as-I'm-told husband type, spoke of our healthy marriage. Randi, the communication-savvy wife, said something like, "Ray is right: We do have a great relationship. I've learned to accept certain parts of his personality that might bother other women."

Her interest piqued, the social worker leaned forward, inquiring, "For instance?"

Randi: "Well, he lies."

In those days I was an inveterate softball player who not uncommonly told Randi, "I'll be home right after the game." Sometimes, though, the guys and I got into analyzing each and every play, so "right after" became "after." Randi and I both knew this to be the "lie" she was referring to, and it was not really a trouble spot in our marriage, at least as I saw it. I think Randi couldn't resist making her psychologist hubby squirm.

The screener had a chuckle, and in her report she recommended a brief stint in an integrity support group, which I'm scheduled to complete sometime next year.

Perhaps an area of particular uncertainty for many is child rearing. Nearly every screener will ask about one's views on parenting and discipline, and nearly every prospective parent will wonder, "What should I say? What if I'm not sophisticated enough kid-wise? What if I come off as too authoritative or too strict? Should I talk about spanking at all?" After all, most folks screened don't have kids yet.

My suggestion? Talk honestly about your philosophy and ideas as they exist right now. Don't be afraid to share how you were raised, especially if you now see it as full of wisdom. Most of the day-to-day stuff of kid raising is grounded in good sense. You don't need to display a high level of psychological enlightenment to come across as a levelheaded, open-to-learning prospective mom or dad.

My first piece of advice to you? Come straight home after the game.

If the impending home study is more worrisome to you than softball, here's a second suggestion: Be yourself. (I get paid for this.) Assuming you have nothing to hide or fear, your openness will not get you into adoption trouble. An experienced evaluator recognizes the wide diversity of folks wanting to adopt and doesn't try to force them into a psychologically narrow mold.

Relax. (Another suggestion born of elite professional training.) Enjoy the opportunity to talk about your thoughts and feelings on a variety of life topics. Indeed, when was the last time someone was interested enough to ask you all about yourself for several hours? I'm confident that once you get past your initial wariness, you'll find the whole process tolerable, even pleasant.

Ask my wife. Would I lie to you?

: : :

NOT A PRETTY PICTURE

Dear Dr. Ray: My wife and I are going through parenting classes at a local agency, as we are hoping to adopt an older child. I'll admit, I'm getting less enthusiastic about the idea, as the classes almost seem to want to frighten us with ugly possibilities.

—*Scared Enough*

I attended a few similar classes myself—as a student, not a teacher—and got the same sense you are getting. Some pretty disconcerting scenarios were presented, from others' past experience and from people's *what-ifs?*

The natural question is, why are such classes recommended? If people want to adopt older children, why on earth would anyone want to discourage them? It's hard enough to find folks who will even consider giving a home to an older child. What's the sense in accosting them with scary pictures?

Are you familiar with the military philosophy underlying basic training? The weeks spent shaping raw recruits into soldiers aren't only to establish self-discipline and obedience to authority. They also serve as a weeding-out process. The aim in putting soldiers-to-be through a grueling, grilling regime of physical and emotional duress is to sort those likely to handle the intensity of actual combat from those not. Put another way, it is to assess whom the heat will melt and whom it will harden.

There is a parallel, I think, to your classes. Adopting older kids isn't combat—really it isn't. Still, one has to have the right mind-set. As far as possible the prospective parent has to be trained and prepared for what might lie ahead. Particularly in parenting, forewarned is forearmed.

Compassion moves many to adopt older children. These parents' hearts are ready to sacrifice and show love to a child who may not have known much. While their motives are unquestionably good, it is their softness itself that can block their view of the future. They are more than willing to give a home but less able to anticipate any complications.

For example, what if the child initially is not pleased to be where she is? What if there are emotional or behavior explosions? What if it takes longer to bond with the child than the couple anticipated? What if the child is years behind in proper socialization? What if the siblings are slow to accept the newcomer?

Adoption specialists are acutely aware that these and other issues can surface after a placement, sometimes emotionally rocking the family. The "horror stories" they present may be a way to psychologically ready parents to stand strong and persevere. Call this a sort of adoption boot camp, training for the special forces of parenthood.

But do these specialists have to be so hard-hitting? If these scenarios are not givens but maybes, couldn't the details be toned down?

In fact, caseworkers do try to give their best assessment of what may or may not be. They don't exaggerate to frighten away all but the most resolute. But exploring particular outcomes and their specifics prompts some parents to react with, "I didn't even consider that." Again, better to be ready for the possible, even if it never becomes actual, than to be unraveled by the unexpected.

One more possibility: A very sad experience for all involved is what adoption professionals call a "disrupted adoption." Here the parents, after the youngster has been in the home for a time, continually presenting major adjustment problems, decide they can no longer continue with the adoption. It has placed excessive stress upon them or their other children, stress they've concluded is not manageable, even with professional support. Occasionally this happens after the court has declared the adoption final, and the child is legally and fully in the family.

Tragically, there are kids who have had more than one failed placement. Most commonly these are very troubled youngsters, whose history is known to the adoptive parents. But with each disruption a child can become emotionally more distant and harder to place with any family.

It is my experience that adoption workers routinely, and wisely, do and say what they can beforehand to lower the chances of a disruption. They know which kids are most at risk because they know their stories. Likewise, the more the parents know what has been, the better they can weather it and adapt if it comes again.

Perhaps your classes are using a worst-case-scenario approach. If you are still eager to adopt after all you've heard, then the everydayness of fatherhood will be a nap in a hammock. OK, I exaggerate. Maybe I should teach some adoption classes.

: : :

HOME FOR GOOD

Dear Dr. Ray: How common is it for the court to return a child to a birth parent or other relative after placement with adoptive parents?

—Looking Over My Shoulder

A few select, high-profile media stories might give the impression that this is a routine adoption risk. Fortunately for adoptive parents everywhere, the image doesn't reflect the reality. The chances of a placement's being reversed because a birth parent or relative seeks it are remote.

But it can happen, can't it? Yes, but the circumstances are not standard to adoption.

To illustrate, suppose early in a placement a birth relative brings forth some sort of legal contention. The situation may then have to be reviewed, perhaps while the child remains with the prospective adoptive parents. Depending upon the complexities of the case, a final decision could take weeks, maybe longer. If the court ultimately rules in favor of the birth family—whatever members that might involve—the temporary placement is then terminated. All along the adoptive parents have realized that challenges were being raised. This is not a surprise coming out of nowhere long after they were settled securely into their adoption.

Awareness of some basic adoption legalities will allay your anxieties.

First of all, the courts are scrupulous in establishing that each birth parent and, where appropriate, other relatives are crystal clear about their rights, options and the consequences of their decisions. The law mandates steps to ensure that any questions or confusion on the part of all parties are addressed. Should a birth parent have second thoughts after the court's decision, significant conditions would have to be met before reconsidering the placement. It is not simply a matter of the birth mom's saying, "I've thought it over some more, and I have changed my mind."

Courts and agencies are acutely conscious of the powerful, sometimes conflicting attitudes and feelings that accompany any adoption. So they make certain that all decisions are fully informed ones, thus dramatically reducing the chances of misunderstanding and future legal issues. In short, once a placement is made appropriately, it becomes a formidable legal process to undo.

Second, many, if not most, adoptions involve a change of custody from an agency to adoptive parents. In other words, the child is already by law in the agency's care, sometimes by a birth parent's choice, other times because of forced removal due to abuse or neglect. Much of the legal *i*-dotting and *t*-crossing occurred when the child was placed by the court with the agency.

In my home state of Ohio, there is a thirty-day placement appeal period. That is, any member of the birth family who wishes to contest the agency's removal and subsequent custody has thirty days to do so. After that time no challenges by birth family members for any reason whatsoever are permitted. The child is in the full custody of the agency. No future adoptive parent has any legal worry at all over challenges to their adoption on the part of the birth family.

Other states vary in their laws regarding the process and time limits for an appeal. For peace of mind, you can easily get such information from your particular agency or attorney.

The end result of all this legal conscientiousness is that, except in the most unusual circumstances, adoptions proceed without complications. While adoptive parents have understandable concerns about what could go awry, the reversal of a placement need not be high on their list.

If you're set on being unsettled anyway, worry about something far more likely to happen, like several months of disrupted sleep. Then there's Grandma's determination to haul thirty stuffed animals into your house. Can you persuade her to rethink her placement of the stuffed stuff? Now, that could be a battle needing a team of lawyers.

:   :   :

Unexpected Visitors

Dear Dr. Ray: We adopted our son, age four, at birth. We've sent pictures to his birth mom yearly. Recently her parents asked to be allowed personal visits. We're reluctant.

—*Surely Unsure*

Yours represents one of the more delicate scenarios in adoption. It doesn't arise all that often, but when it does, it raises disconcerting questions and anxieties for adoptive parents.

When an adoption has had some openness from the outset, occasionally birth parents or members of their families propose new terms of contact. What was once thought settled looks to be changing, unexpectedly. Wherever humans are, change is—in circumstances, emotions, minds. Less contact doesn't unsettle adoptive parents as much as the other way around: More contact arouses the greater uncertainties.

Central to easing your anxieties is this reality: You are the parent. The decision over what to do about this new request is yours to make. In the end you must judge what will be the best resolution for all involved.

That said, asking a number of questions may help shape your final answer. Some of these questions can be definitively answered, and others elicit only best guesses. Nevertheless they need to be asked, and the most accurate answers possible discerned.

To begin, how open has the adoption been up to now? If there has been an ongoing personal relationship with a birth parent or relatives, adding a couple more contacts may not change your family scenery much. The child is likely accustomed to a somewhat fluid arrangement of birth and adoptive relatives.

Since your current arrangement consists only of regular pictures, I'm assuming there have been no personal contacts at all. Introducing another set of grandparents, brand-new ones, could confuse your son. What will he make of this redrawn family picture and how it all fits in with the grandparents he has?

Then again, is the birth mom asking for visitation? In any less-to-more-contact scenario, all other things being equal, she deserves first consideration. Even if her parents have the stronger desire to stay connected, they are still further removed from the adoption than she. Put simply, if an adoption arrangement is going to be altered, the birth mom most often gets first voice.

What are the grandparents like? What do you know about their personalities, emotional stability, relationship with the birth mom? What is their reason for seeking contact now, four years after your child's birth? The less you know about them, the more caution you should exercise in connecting them with your son. Before a parent opens any door for a child, he needs a really good idea of what's behind that door.

Do you have a sense of the grandparents' level of future cooperation with you? Your conditions, expectations and limits must be respected. In any visitation you set the terms. Are you reasonably confident, at least as far as now knowable, that your parameters will be acceptable? And what if they're not? Can you extricate yourself from a situation turned sour? One of the last things you want to invite is ongoing conflict over what you think are reasonable terms for contact.

What about gifts and goodies? Grandparents of all types are noted for dispensing too much stuff, even more so than parents these days. Can you assess what their style might be? Will it be a weekly Toys-R-Us truck? A modest U-Haul trailer? An M&M candy split in half?

Continuing with the questions—don't you hate it when shrinks do that?—how much and how long do the birth grandparents want to be involved? For childhood? For life? Will visitations all occur at your home? Any at theirs? Will the visits be supervised? What if any social activities or entertainment will be involved? With anyone else? Where? Are any half siblings, now or someday, to be included? Will the birth mom be introduced at some point?

Obviously, any initial reassurances may not reflect eventual reality. At the least you need to make clear your terms up front. Introducing these matters and observing the grandparents' reactions to them should give you some inkling of what could unfold. My aim is not to make your decision impossible. It is to raise questions about the possible. Your son has a stable image of who his family is. Adding more people to the photo, introducing them as "other family" or "more grandparents," may be easier for your grown-up mind to assimilate than his little one.

From your question I don't know if you have other children, birth or adopted. If you do your situation becomes even more complex. The other kids might raise questions. Who are these people? How long are they going to be around? Are they just my brother's grandparents or sort of mine too? Do I visit with them? Do I stay out of the way because they are only interested in my brother? If you all go to the park to meet them, do I go too?

Such inquiries may be more or less troubling for siblings. Whatever perplexes your son will probably perplex his siblings, even if less so.

Perhaps the most intricate scenario involves one or more adopted siblings. Here a sibling's circumstances parallel the brother's closely. "Do I have other grandparents out there somewhere too? Why can't I see them? Will I ever get to see them? Maybe I like the ones I have; do I have to get new ones?"

Kids learn early how to do social arithmetic. They add two plus two in life and get four long before they can do so with numbers. If I have grandparents, maybe I have brothers and sisters. How about another mom? Maybe they know where I am? What if there's a whole bunch of people I'm not seeing?

These are legitimate, honest questions that adopted kids may ask at any time. In and of themselves they are not necessarily distressing. The main issue lies in the timing. Your child's questions might be stimulated sooner, perhaps at a much younger age than you'd want. As his parent, while you are prepared to respond when the questions arise, in your judgment it may not be good to introduce them at age five or eight or even ten. Someday you will, but you hope it is after your son has had years to settle into who he is in the family and who his family is.

You are not looking to dodge tough questions. You're looking to answer them at a time most meaningful, and least confusing, to your son.

So am I warning, "Don't do it"? No, I am not. As I said before I started raising so many questions, the final answer is yours. Still, it doesn't take a psychologist to sense my reservations over your circumstances.

This new contact might look beneficial, and birth grandparents might present as sweet people. Still, there are many unknowns to be acknowledged, anticipated and where possible answered. The core of the matter is not what is best for the birth grandparents, as kind and reasonable as they might be, but what's ultimately best for your son, you and everyone else close to your family.

chapter five

ADOPTION RESISTANCE

It's human nature. If we think something is good, if we pursue it, we want others to agree with it or at least to accept it. Adoption is something that can emotionally move a person quickly and deeply. Therefore it's natural for us to hope that others, particularly those closest to us, share our feelings, at least somewhat anyway.

Alas, this is not always so. Family members especially, because they are most directly affected, may be the most reluctant or resistant. Some might think, "This is your idea, not mine." Can they be influenced to rethink their perspective?

Two potent factors are on your side to help you persuade others: time and a child.

: : :

A HOUSE DIVIDED

Dear Dr. Ray: I want to adopt. My spouse is resistant. What do you do in a situation like this?

—*Vote?*

Nothing. Not yet anyway.

Adoption is one of those big family decisions that need a meeting of two adult minds, at least partway. The kids' minds are another matter, one we'll probe in a few pages.

I don't know what you mean by "resistant." Is it "absolutely not"? Is it "I'm not as enthusiastic about this as you are"? Is it "I'm willing but not right now"? How about "I'm willing, but I'm not sure you're able"?

To encourage you, I've known spouses to rethink their position over time, going from negative to neutral to positive. Or they agree to adopt with less than full enthusiasm, only to grow comfortably into being a mother or father, for the first time or once again. Believe it or not, there are even those whose reluctance for one child has evolved into a wish for more, as that first child has altered their whole outlook.

This said, let's assess your present situation. Is it "absolutely not, no way, no how"? Then better not to push too hard or relentlessly, especially if doing so will hurt your marriage. In the long run your best ally in making yourself heard is a healthy marriage, one that eases disagreements over time. If your spouse is well aware of your strong desire to adopt, hammering away at the subject will probably harden, not soften that position. Let agitated feelings settle. Allow your reasons to soak in, if at all possible.

In short, give the matter some rest between revisits. As I said, adoption is a decision that needs dual consent, even if one party's is with reservations.

What if your spouse's attitude is "I'm not as enthusiastic about this as you are"? That's OK. Routinely husbands and wives aren't at the same level of agreement, preference or priority for a lot of things, most of which are simpler than a child. If you have other children, ask your spouse if his or her love for them has grown over the years. (Make sure it has before you ask!) Why wouldn't love grow similarly with another child?

If you have no children, refer to the observations made in a previous question, "Number, Please?"—that is, the rewards of a child are only fully experienced by actually having a child. The idea of a first child often breeds more ambivalence than the reality. Once the child arrives, the initial questions and worries quickly begin to dissolve.

Reassure your spouse that you are fully aware that he or she doesn't have your attraction to this whole idea, and you don't expect that right now. Further, as long as your spouse acknowledges having mixed feelings on the subject, you've got some common ground for discussion. Talk first about that on which you agree.

"I'm willing but not right now." Find out why, without getting defensive or arguing. Spend whatever time needed to seek and listen to any reasons your spouse has for being reluctant to adopt. Don't challenge; don't debate; just nudge your spouse to be as open as possible in expressing thoughts about it. In essence you're doing what a good therapist does. You are seeking to know in detail what is inside another's mind and heart.

Am I saying you should never offer answers to your spouse's reasons? No, in due time you can explain yourself (again?). What I am saying is first to listen, ask questions and strive to understand—no matter how disappointing, shortsighted or ridiculous your spouse's reasons seem. Before you can share your own thoughts, you must make certain you know your spouse's.

The "I'm willing, but you're not able" could be the perception easiest to change, as long as you're willing to change too. It requires exploring exactly why your spouse believes you would struggle with adopting and raising a child. Are you home too little? Are your discipline skills weak? Do you complain about being stressed with life now? Are you poorly organized? Are you too extravagant materially?

Make a connubial deal: Ask your spouse for six months to prove that you can change what seem to be obstacles to adopting. If in fact you do better, you've made a powerful counter-argument.

What if the improvement isn't enough for your spouse? Ask for another six months. After all, you are trending in the right direction. And if your spouse's objections are legitimate, you need to change anyway, with or without another child.

If your spouse's arguments are counterfeits for the real reason —"I don't want to"—your genuine attempts to improve yourself may yet soften him or her. Your spouse is seeing every day in your behavior how much this means to you.

If your spouse still doesn't care to adopt, you may have to ultimately accept that. Few things in life feel as futile as struggling to persuade someone who strongly disagrees with you, especially on emotional subjects. (If you have a teenager, you know first-hand this frustration.)

Nevertheless, you've got a few starting points. Persevere, and who knows, you could see your feelings about adoption start to build in your spouse.

:   :   :

A Two-Hundred-Grand Kid

Dear Dr. Ray: My husband recently read an article claiming that the cost of raising a child to age eighteen is two hundred thousand dollars. That pushed him further away from the adoption idea.

—Loan Arranger

Those kinds of articles scare me. If my kids ever got hold of those figures, they'd feel mighty shortchanged. My seventeen-year-old daughter would probably present me with a balance due bill of $123,000 on her eighteenth birthday.

I've always been fascinated by the guesstimates of child-raising costs. The numbers vary wildly, depending, it would seem, upon the author's idea of what all is needed materially to properly bring up a youngster. Is it clothes from Maurice's European Fashions or Joe's Thrice-Worn Jeans? Public or private schools? Semi-annual vacations to Disney World or a yearly camping trip in the woods two miles from one's back door? Personal computer, TV, iPod, cell phone, four-wheeler—all presented by age twelve? A driver's license and car at age sixteen or a weekly bus token?

The variability in cost per kid per parent per lifestyle is enormous. So such figures are at the least questionable and at the worst misleading.

The basics—food, shelter, clothing, transportation, education, medical and dental care, insurance—at some level are nonnegotiable. But even they can fluctuate widely.

What kinds of food, and how much? At-home meals or drive-through? How often?

How many square feet of house per child? One bedroom per kid, or one bunk bed per two kids?

What about the ratio of brand-new stuff to older stuff? A new (or used) bike every four years or every year?

In our family, I'll admit, the food bill is a little overwhelming, especially as the kids get older. A friend offered one cost-cutting solution: boys eat Monday, Wednesday and Friday; girls— Tuesday, Thursday, Saturday; Sunday is family day, and everybody eats. That idea didn't get too far with my wife. Randi's really into the nutrition thing, no matter the cost.

Our oldest child was the clothing pioneer. Andrew got more first-time outfits than any of the other nine. Our last, Elizabeth, would be ecstatic to have a sweater passed down only twice.

Barring exceptional circumstances, each additional child costs less than the preceding. The oldest has already accumulated for any siblings many of the everyday child-rearing necessities. Further, added kids inhale the same air, use most of the same electricity and heat, share toys (under duress) and cost less in private school tuition due to family discounts. Two driving-aged teens can use the same car, however brutal such a deprivation might seem in their eyes.

Bottom line? What each child costs is dramatically affected by the control and judgment of the parents. A quarter-million dollars might run out for some families by the time the first child hits fourth grade, while carrying others through two or three kids.

What's more, once the material basics are met, I'm convinced there is little relationship between the maturity and morality of the child and the level of "good living." No, I take that back. There *is* a relationship: The more excessive the indulgence, the less likely good morals and maturity.

Is your husband reluctant to adopt for reasons other than financial? If so, then the money is an added justification for something he isn't enthused about anyway. All your financial reassuring may not answer the essence of his resistance. To do that, refer to some of the other questions in this book.

On the other hand, if his anxiety is primarily money-rooted, he might be settled some by these counterarguments. Perhaps the real question comes down to "What price would deter you from adopting?" If even a little of him is leaning toward adoption, then more realistic figures may inflate his yes and deflate his no.

If you can get your husband to settle on a concrete figure, you could present him with an eighteen-year budget estimate. (The government does it.) Or you could tell him you'll take out a loan or get a night job to save up the first three years of costs. At the risk of sounding even crasser, over eighteen years the tax credits and individual deductions, even if they stay at current levels, will save you about $40,000 in total taxes. So the $200,000 gross cost is really $160,000 net. The savings could be enough for funding another kid through kindergarten.

Actually, when all is paid and done, the main issue lies in your husband's view of kids and adoption compared to yours. To the degree that his inclination to adopt increases, his financial concerns will decrease. In the end, even if the grand total comes in at $212,743.22, he will consider it a small price for something of infinite value.

: : :

THREE'S COMPANY, FOUR'S A CROWD

Dear Dr. Ray: My husband and I want to adopt, but my seven-year-old daughter is very upset at the idea. She's gotten pretty comfortable with our family being just the three of us.

—*Growing Pained*

If you were hoping to get pregnant, would you first seek your daughter's permission? If you've been trying to conceive for the last several years, have you been annually asking her if it's still OK? What about a career change? Does she agree? How about moving to a different home? Changing the wallpaper in the bathroom? Changing the TV channel? Changing lanes?

OK, not all of these impact your daughter equally. The TV channel switch might provoke the most distress, depending upon the show. Still, you get the point. Most big family decisions are primarily yours and your spouse's to make. You're older, smarter, more experienced, and you have a much better eye for what pattern will best go with your countertop.

I once read a counselor's advice to a parent not to adopt because her daughter was against it. His logic was that this was a family matter, the child's feelings were important and needed to be heard, and given how strongly she felt, she should have the authority to veto the whole idea. Note: This was a ten-year-old—the kid, not the expert.

I'm with him on three of four. Of course, the child's or children's opinions count. Though I wonder, how many kids have to vote nay on an adoption before it's defeated? Do all members of the family have an equal say? If so, my wife and I risked never adopting again after our first three children. Thank goodness, we could bribe them at their young ages. A few M&M's, and magic—a raised hand for a brother.

Just teasing. They're not that shallow. It took a banana milk-shake too.

Ideally all children—the older ones particularly—would feel part of the discussion. And if any are cool toward the idea, certainly hear them out and attempt to reassure, persuade, educate. Try the jumbo banana shake with the added syrup.

Where that counselor and I part ways rapidly is on his last point: A child has the power to sway the whole adoption decision. Most kids are either neutral or pretty excited about a new sibling, however he might arrive. There are those, though, who are vehemently opposed to new family members. They like home life just the way it is, thank you. In their heads all kinds of negative scenarios arise when they consider having another person—baby or older—enter their world.

Psychological studies have shown that adults are not very good at predicting beforehand how they will behave in actual situations when they arise. Recall the question in the first chapter, "Number, Please?"—the observation was made that routinely parents underestimate the power of their feelings for a child until after they have one. Or they worry needlessly that their love for a yet-to-be second child might not reach the level held for the first.

If an adult, who has had decades of getting to know himself and his tendencies, can misjudge his reactions, how accurate can one expect a child to be about his or her behavior before a situation presents itself? Quite simply, your daughter has little idea how she and her new sibling ultimately will relate.

Children are not good judges of what is good for them. That's why we parent types compel them against their will to do all manner of things—finish chores, eat right, complete school-work, dress appropriately, use manners, be respectful, be nice to siblings. In time most kids come to understand the good in what they initially resisted. They're even grateful for having been forced.

If you believe your family will be a better place for all by adding another member, then act. Trust that your daughter will more than merely adapt to her new family; she will come to experience firsthand what she couldn't understand in her head. Once her brother or sister is here a while, she will be glad she was not permitted to overrule Mom and Dad.

: : :

OUT OF THE RUINS

Dear Dr. Ray: We recently adopted a little boy, age three, who is a handful. Our five-year-old daughter seems to be accepting him pretty well, but our nine-year-old daughter sees him as an intruder. The other day she even said to me, "Why did you ruin our family?"

—Did I?

Kids can be so childish—they see things through the prism of how they affect them. They're slow to grasp the bigger picture. And they don't realize that time can alter initial impressions for the better.

Wait a minute—adults do that too. The only difference is that kids generally are quicker to change an attitude from poor to positive.

No surprise that children in a family differ, sometimes dramatically, in how they welcome a new sibling, natural or adopted. Accepting a baby is child's play for most kids, especially older ones. Babies aren't very threatening. Their behavior doesn't actively engage or deliberately provoke other children in the house. For several weeks or so, they just lie around and leak out of body openings.

Introduce an older child into the family, and you introduce a new personality and interactive style, to use a fancy phrase. He or she can agitate or inflame any of the other already established personalities in the house.

You know your daughters. Most likely you could have predicted which one was more likely to resist a new preschool brother, based upon her age, self-perceived family status, temperament, sociability. Whatever your nine-year-old's struggles now, they aren't necessarily good predictors of future sibling ties. Way too much will unfold to be able to forecast how close the kids will be years, even months from now.

In fact, your nine-year-old could grow fonder of her little brother, while your five-year-old could start to clash with him because of their closer ages. There, don't you feel better? Just trying to help.

As I've shared, we adopted our twins, Jonathan and Joanna, at age four. Andrew, age six, was ecstatic to have a brother big enough to play with, yet still thump, in sports. Hannah, age five, was thrilled to have two more siblings to rule. Sammy, age one, was vaguely aware that there were more bodies to bump into.

The big adjustment came with Sarah, age three. These two newcomers were a little too near her age for Sarah's liking. And there was no hiding of her three-year-old feelings. She began to bite, not just the twins but anyone else who came near her fangs. She also was quick to express her opinion of our decision to expand the family. Once we caught her hissing at Joanna, "You're going back!" Clearly Sarah did not want these children in our home. (I noticed this only because I'm a trained professional.)

How long did Sarah take to accept the fact that the twins were staying, despite her vote, and to feel warmth toward them? Acceptance? Several months. Warmth? We hope by next year. Just teasing. Sarah and Jo came to be buds—buddettes?—within the first year, and throughout adolescence both often said the other was her best friend.

No doubt your daughter presently has some strong feelings. Her nine-year-old mind isn't sure where this brother thing is headed. She liked the family the old way; it was what she knew. However shortsighted she is, her emotions are very real to her.

Therefore, I suggest that you continue to talk with her, asking her all about her views. Reassure her that you and Dad won't be splitting up your love but that you will now love *all* of your children more. Children multiply love; they don't divide it. She'll find that out.

Your daughter's reaction toward her brother is understandable, even acceptable for a time. Any negative behavior is not. I can't emphasize this enough. *Do not* allow her to act on her feelings. Stop her and discipline her if necessary. It is one thing to have inhospitable feelings; it is quite another to demonstrate those feelings.

If she is disciplined "because of" her brother, couldn't she just resent him even more? Short answer: No. Longer answer: If someone mistreats another in the name of authentic feelings, does this help or hurt their relationship over time? Not only will your daughter continue to recharge her own negativity, but little brother may start to retaliate with meanness of his own. Then you will have two kids mistreating one another. That won't do much to smooth any transition.

If your daughter is not permitted to act out her adoption resistance, her intense initial feelings could cool for lack of fuel. Further, given that she will be living in the same house as her brother—you do plan to keep her, don't you?—the natural everyday sibling interactions will gradually lead to a better relationship. When a child isn't allowed to torment a sibling, she basically has two options: (1) learn to get along with the sibling; (2) ignore the sibling. Most kids gravitate toward the former, as there is too much everyday contact to readily permit the latter.

Standard expert advice in these scenarios also includes: (1) emphasize your daughter's special status as the big sister of a now bigger family; (2) involve her where you can in the caretaking or, when appropriate, the decision making regarding her little brother; (3) set up situations in which she shares a privilege or activity with him; (4) allow her to show this new kid on the block exactly who has been running the neighborhood for the past nine years. OK, this last one isn't really common expert advice; I just threw it in to see if you are paying attention.

As grown-ups mesh more or less well with other personalities, so too do kids. Even if at first you have to make your daughter treat her brother OK, the chances are very good that she'll come to see in time that he's an OK kid. She'll learn firsthand that you didn't ruin her family; you made it bigger and better.

: : :

Too Many Children?

Dear Dr. Ray: We have three birth children, ages ten, eight and four. We are thinking about adopting, preferably an infant, but some of our relatives (read: "parents") are questioning us. They say our plate is already full, and they worry that the adoption will "take away" from our other kids.

—*Relatively Speaking*

There is a phenomenon widespread, tragic even, in parenting today. I suspect it's never before occurred in human history. Parents who want more than two children face an increasing fusillade of comments, criticism and callous remarks from others, often their own relatives.

"Do you know how this is happening?" "Don't you have a TV?" "Are they all yours?" "Are you done yet?" "You really do have your hands full." "Well, you have a boy and a girl, so this is it, right?" "I'm sure glad it's you and not me." On this last one a mother told me she responded, "I think my kids are too."

A father once shared with me that after their first several children, neither he nor his wife any longer announced, "We're pregnant," to most friends and colleagues. They simply were tired of the barrage of negative and perplexed reactions.

Many mothers have told me that upon their third pregnancy, out came the pamphlets from their doctors or nurses instructing them how to avoid another pregnancy. The pamphlets were not requested.

What an astounding commentary on the perceived value of offspring today! The attitude seems to be, children are a good thing, as long as their numbers are limited, say, to two or under per family. What's more, it is now seen as acceptable, even proper, to offer an "enlightened" opinion on whether or not someone should have another child. While this attitude is most voiced toward pregnancies over two, parents who already have their allowable quota of children, and who now wish to expand their family through adoption, also face it.

To give your relatives the benefit of the doubt, let's assume that their motive is well intentioned. They are genuinely concerned about your parenting load, and their lack of support for your adoption comes from that. If you had no children, or even one, they would be excited for you. But as they see it, you have a family—a large one—so why do you need more children? Why shake things up? Adoption is great for those who can't get pregnant, but why are you chasing this idea? Far better for you, and the kids, to leave well enough alone.

Neither you nor I agree with their view, but we can acknowledge it.

Ironically, though, the most reluctant grandparents sometimes had five, six or more children themselves. And generally they raised them with far fewer resources—material and otherwise—than today's parents enjoy.

How then do you get your extended family to think differently? In the short term, you probably can't. Right now it's hard for them to be enthusiastic about your adoption because any new child is just an idea. He or she is not real yet—no kid antics, no cute face, no kisses for Grandma.

Your biological children are here and now. They have a relationship, a mutual attachment to your parents. They are already family. Put another way, the competition is unfair. It pits the present against the future, the known versus the unknown, the already loved against the yet to be accepted.

There is hope. Probably the best way to relax your parents' resistance to your adopting is to adopt. Let a child slowly win them over. Show them that their fears are unfounded. Another child hasn't subtracted from your first children; he has added. Your family is becoming even more familylike.

Of course, this may take some time, years maybe. There could be setbacks or "I told you so's" should there be adjustment troubles. Nonetheless, even the most adoption-wary relatives, in my experience, are not hard-hearted. Eventually most soften to the whole adoption idea, because they soften toward the child, or children.

Worst case scenario: What if they don't? What if they always view your adopted son or daughter as a sort of a second-class citizen, not a genuine member of the family?

That possibility alone would not be enough to make me second-guess my desire to adopt. First of all, plenty enough love will come from you, your kids and other relatives to welcome and assimilate this new child. Second, while acceptance from everyone would be great, it isn't necessary to a child's adjustment. It may create some questions or struggles for you to address in coming years. Still, no relative has the power to keep me from adopting if that is what I want to do.

What about the child? What if he feels the discrimination coming from Grandpa or Aunt Patience? Again, that's where a good parent comes in. You're there to help your child see that this is the other person's problem, not the child's. The attitude is neither a good nor a mature one, and it has absolutely nothing to do with who the child is or how much you and others in the family want him.

Let's repeat: Not all may understand or support your decision to adopt. Sometimes those disagreeing most loudly are close relatives. Most often the adoptee will win them over in time, as they come to know and love her. Even if not, never let the opinions of others overrule your decision to adopt. The full favor of all may be ideal; it is not critical to the well-being of your child. Your love and that of others will more than compensate for what's lacking elsewhere.

:   :   :

THE CINDERELLA SYNDROME

Dear Dr. Ray: A close relative (grandfather) did not and does not accept our nine-year-old son, adopted at age two. He is cordial to him but clearly favors our two younger, biological children.

—*What Now?*

As I've said prior to this, time and a child often soften a hard attitude toward an adoption. Sometimes, though, a long time—in your case seven years—and the sweetest child doesn't noticeably change a heart. What then?

Let's begin with Grandpa. Has he ever made clear to you exactly why he treats the kids differently? Or have you had to cobble together your impressions through bits of his behavior and comments he's made over the years? More often than not, the latter is so, as family members typically aren't blatant about deep negative feelings, especially if somewhere deeper they realize those feelings shouldn't be there.

Although several years in the making, it's still not too late to explore further what's influencing Grandpa. If he's your father, you'd probably best take the lead in approaching, or as it may be, reapproaching the subject. As a rule, a son or daughter, as opposed to an in-law, is in a better position to tread on touchy turf.

Your goal is, without argument or ill will, to ask questions in order to gain a better grasp of the situation. Don't challenge or correct yet. You're aiming to understand more fully.

Maybe Grandpa will resist talking about it. Maybe he'll dispute or minimize your observations. Maybe he'll get defensive within the first question or two. Nevertheless, your hope is to uncover, if at all possible, what he is thinking and feeling regarding your son as well as your other two children. My experience as a therapist is that folks on the receiving end of questionable or hurtful treatment often don't have a good notion of the *why* behind it.

In the most positive outcome, your father (or father-in-law) will clarify for you the reasons for his attitude. This will bring about two benefits:

One, you will know better how to help your son comprehend his grandfather. Better understanding leads to less guesswork and confusion, for you and him.

Two, your frustration level may be lowered some. How so? Even if you don't agree with Grandpa, any contrition or regrets he admits may soothe your feelings. Listening to another struggle with his weakness does tend to ease our upset at that weakness. Who knows, you may be surprised to find that Grandpa doesn't like how he's acted. Time has in fact been softening him, however agonizingly slowly.

If none of the above transpires, at the very least Grandpa is now fully aware that you are fully aware of this family dynamic. You, your spouse and perhaps your son feel it. Even the younger grandchildren may be starting to notice. Sometimes when behavior is out in the open, it's harder to maintain. There's no more denying it exists.

What about your son? How much you discuss with him depends upon how much he notices or, if he notices, how much it affects him. Understandably, you probably hurt more than he does. You're his parent, his protector. Nevertheless, don't point out the partiality if he isn't aware of it. No sense bringing to light what he blissfully doesn't see yet. Let him reside a while longer in his childhood innocence.

On the other hand, if your son senses any inequity, one or more conversations may be in order, focusing on a few key points. First and foremost, he is not the cause of Grandpa's conduct; Grandpa is. Whatever Grandpa thinks about him or his adoption may be partly or all wrong. Help him understand and accept the fact that just because somebody is a "grown-up" doesn't mean he will always act well or right. Put simply, grown-up may better describe their age than their behavior.

Second, Grandpa may or may not change. Time will tell. You may have to temper your son's expectations of Grandpa. Yes, it would be great if Grandpa were fair and even across kids, but that's not the case. Lowered expectations will lead to less disappointment and frustration.

What about Grandpa's favoritism toward your other children? Here you may have to go beyond words to action. You might not be able to stop Grandpa from making remarks, giving unequal affection or expressing preferential emotions. But you can put limits on overt, blatant favoritism. For example, Grandpa won't be permitted to take your birth children to a ball game, leaving behind your adopted son, or head out for pizza with only two of the three kids or obviously differ in the kind and number of birthday and Christmas gifts. It is one thing to feel partiality; it is quite another to freely and openly display that partiality.

What if Grandpa persists with his sliding scale for gifts, money and social outings? Gifts can be divided equally later or given away. Toys can become community property. Holiday money can be disbursed fairly, even if not so given. Social outings may have to proceed from a simple rule: All go or no one goes.

In essence, as parents you will steadfastly correct any deliberate, obvious material or social favoritism. Your actions will convey a clear message: We all are of equal status and dignity in this family, no matter how anyone—family members too—treats us. No child can benefit at the expense of a sibling.

Will your younger kids understand? Probably not fully, given their ages. As they mature, though, they will come to see that their brother deserves fairness. In time they may even begin to resist their artificially elevated family positions.

Within my list of suggestions, have you noticed one option conspicuously absent? That is, if Grandpa doesn't soften his ways, what about prohibiting contact with his grandchildren? My reasons for avoiding such advice?

Given all the grandparent-parent-grandchild complications possible, rare is the dynamic so bad that all contact has to be severed. Certainly in cases of abuse, malicious mistreatment or blatant undercutting of a parent's authority, separation may be the final option. However, in the more routine cases of discipline differences, personality conflicts or preferential treatment, terminating a relationship might be called the nuclear option.

First of all, seldom does it improve strained relationships. The chasm separating family members only becomes deeper.

Misunderstandings and misread motives multiply with time. All too often the estrangement becomes prolonged, removing further any hope of reconciliation, even if one or both parties would consider it.

Second, how can healing occur without contact? No contact means no relationship. And it is only in the context of a relationship, which for sure isn't always negative, that bad feelings can slowly be shifted. Build upon what's good in your relationship with Grandpa, and you may watch him reconsider his bad attitude.

Finally, for most kids the presence of a grandparent, however humanly flawed, is a childhood treasure. While we grown-ups may be acutely aware of a relative's imperfections—I wonder how much they could tell us about ours—kids are generally more accepting, if only because they are generally more oblivious. Said simply, kids often have to see a lot of bad stuff before wanting a grandparent gone from their lives.

A final thought: Don't assume Grandpa's feelings are set in stone. Who your son is and who he becomes may yet win his grandfather. Then too, he may get some help from his siblings. Over time they could start sending Grandpa signals to treat their brother right. Who knows, in the end they may be the ones to change Grandpa. After all, it's hard to resist someone you're partial to.

chapter six

COMMUNICATION 101

The adoptive relationship is at once both normal and unique. As such, talking about that relationship with a child or adult can raise uncertainty for many parents. Questions of when, how and how much abound.

Fortunately, the core currency of the adoptive relationship is not words but love. While the words used matter, they are not so critical that one must feel unsure or inept over exactly how to talk about adoption with another, especially a child. Practicing a few basics should make any communication easier and smoother.

: : :

TALK RIGHT

Dear Dr. Ray: I know that most people mean no offense, but I find myself wanting to correct insensitive comments and language like "real parents" or "Who do they look like?" Should I?
—*Language Weary*

Nearly every sphere of life develops its own vocabulary and inner-circle lingo. Psychologically speaking, if I say, "Borderline personality marked by passive aggressive tendencies with potential decompensation to paranoia given acute social exacerbation," you'd probably respond with, "I concur, given past regressive patterns." Then again, maybe you wouldn't.

A more incomprehensible example comes from my thirty-year career playing softball. As a pitcher I might turn to my outfield players and shout my scouting report on the batter: "Give him a step. Good pop both gaps. Bad wheel, but likes to stretch for two. Opposite stripe dead." (I know, you'd rather talk to a psychologist.)

I know what I mean. So do my teammates and the batter. Call it the language of the field, spoken easily by the experienced, unfamiliar to the less involved.

As adoption has become more culturally and cross-culturally common, it too has developed its own vocabulary and, if you will, rules of speaking etiquette. Terms such as "real parents" have been replaced by "birth parents" or "biological parents." "Give up for adoption" is now "place for adoption." "Handicapped child" has become "a child with special needs." In essence the language of adoption, like language in general, is ever-evolving. It has become more accurate and more sensitive.

Nonetheless, just as the nonpsychologist or non–softball player might use less "professional" words in the above situations, so too those not personally acquainted with the world of adoption may use older, less currently acceptable terms. Their language has not kept pace with the latest transitions in words and thinking.

I hope that this will help temper your reactions to what might sound like thoughtless, even callous remarks and questions. Many people simply don't know, nor have they been educated in, better ways to speak about adoption. As you observed, no offense is intended. And it is noticeably easier to calm any urge to react when one does not impart negative motives to another.

Am I advising that you simply smile sweetly, nod agreeably and answer any and all ill-phrased questions? Not at all. I am suggesting you pick and choose when you respond and how.

Merely substituting a better word often teaches well. For example, "Has she ever asked about her real mom?" "No. Up to this point she hasn't asked much about her birth parents." Or if you're pretty quick, "Well, she asks about me a lot, but so far not too much about her birth mom." Or, "What am I? A fake mom?" Use a smile with this last one, or else you could be defensive when nothing offensive was meant.

At times rephrasing a question or comment with better language will gently educate. Every so often it takes a little more. Once at an amusement park ticket booth, my wife was asked by a total stranger—yes, in front of all the children—"What do you think their real mom is thinking right now?" To which my wife replied—and this is why I rarely argue with her—"I'm thinking I'd like ten tickets for this ride."

Sound bites are good ripostes, making a point without belaboring it. For instance, we've heard, "Are they all yours?" Yes, they are all ours. "No, I mean, which ones are yours?" All of them. "But aren't some adopted?" Sure, but they're all ours.

Perhaps part of my relaxed attitude comes from my own "reeducation" at the hands of others. Some years ago I commented to someone about a "special needs child," whereupon she informed me, "child with special needs." Or I've said "black children" and heard "African-American children." On occasion, it must be noted, the language used is neither right nor wrong. It is simply not the other person's preferred phrase. And maybe he is being downright prickly about it. Avoid that attitude in yourself at all costs.

When all is said, however inaccurately, I let most adoption misstatements pass. I agree with you, most people mean no insult. Further, I don't like being a language policeman—I mean, language police person. What educating I do comes primarily from the words I personally use when talking about adoption. And here and there, if I can conjure up a good comeback on the spot, I struggle to stifle myself.

But not always. Once someone was sizing up our many-person family, and I confessed, "I'm afraid to come home and ask my wife, 'What's new?'"

:   :   :

THE ADOPTION TALK(S)

Dear Dr. Ray: My two children, adopted as infants, are now four and one. It's not a concern yet, but how do we tell them of their adoption? We've read so much we're getting more confused.

—When and How?

There's a saying about child-rearing experts: If all were laid end to end, none would point in the same direction. While perhaps a bit of an exaggeration, nevertheless it is a pointed observation. There is no shortage of opinions and ideas lying about, not only in adoption but in parenting in general.

Since you're asking me which way I'd point, I'll answer. Can I stay standing upright?

The adoption talk, or more accurately talks, is something that looms over adoptive parents. It's stamped with question marks. When do I introduce it? How do I? How much detail? How often do I revisit it? Do I take the lead, or does my child?

For all the angst surrounding it, "the talk" is one of the easier discussions of adoptive parenting. How so? Because of the children. Most will offer openings through their everyday conversation. Allow my son Peter to demonstrate.

During his preschool years, regularly Peter and I would meet my parents for breakfast. I don't recall what my mother said to get his five-year-old mind musing, but as we were driving away from the restaurant one day, Peter began.

"Dad, you were in Grandma's belly when you were a really little baby, weren't you?"

"Yes, Petey, I was."

"Was I in Mommy's belly?"

Oh boy, here we go. And I'm in the car, without my wife. Well, I guess now's as good a time as any to talk.

"No, Peter, you weren't. You were in another mommy's belly."

Silence. He was processing. Maybe he would process long enough for me to get home and find Randi. No chance.

"How did I get in there?"

Great. I just dodged the adoption talk only to face the facts-of-life talk. As a shrink I'm trained in communication techniques. When in doubt, seek clarification.

"What do you mean, Pete?"

"You know, who put me in there?"

An accurate answer can always involve God, while ducking unwanted specifics.

"God put you in there."

"How did he do that?"

"What do you mean, Pete?"

I wholeheartedly advise the "What do you mean?" strategy for a range of parent-child discourses.

"I mean, did he throw me down in there, or did he just lay me in there?"

I might make it home after all. Pete was just asking boy-type questions.

"Well, Pete, that's easy. He just laid you in there."

Dead silence. Discussion closed. Peter was satisfied—for one traffic light. Then came his grand finale: "Why didn't she keep me?"

I didn't have my cell phone to call Randi, so it looked as if I was on my own.

"Petey, she wanted you to have a mommy and a daddy, and she didn't have a daddy for you. So she looked for a mommy and a daddy. God knew you needed a daddy, and he also knew I needed a Petey, so he put us together."

Deafening silence, but this time a smile. Then Pete noticed a big tractor-trailer hauling cows, and that ended his queries. By the time we reached home, I was feeling pretty full of myself. I'd handled the whole interchange without once saying, "I think you need to ask Mom about this."

Actually Pete had shown previous curiosity about his origins, but this was his most thoughtful. I am white; Pete is black. While he didn't know much about the birds and bees, he did know his colors. But until that day he never pursued their implications.

Sometimes it's the sight of an expectant mother. Sometimes it's a black child walking with a white parent. Other times it's simply the sight of a baby. Almost anything can prompt a child's adoption questions. And from there the kids will guide us into their thoughts.

What if they never ask any questions? What if the curiosity doesn't percolate?

It may be that none is there yet. Don't feel pressured to chase it. Or if you think it's quietly present, then you can use the sight of a pregnant mom, a baby in a crib or the nursery at church to open up a conversation. You certainly don't need to drag out details for an hour—you would lose most kids' attention long before then—but the discourse usually unfolds smoothly, even if you're not a counselor.

Which leads me to a warning: Resist "psychological correctness," the notion that there are only specific ways to talk about adoption and share, respond and acknowledge feelings. Most parents can read their children well. Guided primarily by instincts and good sense, you decide how best to begin, how far to explore and when to close the subject.

Furthermore, you have a powerful psychological ally: Your children see you and have always seen you as their parent. Any new history they hear will most likely be interpreted in light of what they've known every day since birth: You are my mom (or my dad).

Sometimes older kids have been thinking a while before they speak up. My son Andrew, at about age thirteen, struggling to find his words, asked, "Dad, would you love me more if, well, you know, if I had been ..." Long pause.

"You mean, if you had been born to Mom and me?"

"Yeah, that's it."

"Andrew, who do I love more than anyone in the world?"

"Mom."

Am I glad he got that one right! My wife was listening.

"Am I related to Mom?"

"No, you're not, are you?"

The light went on, and he was settled, at least about that question—whereupon he went outside and threw a ball off the side of the house for an hour.

While that was Andrew's reaction, had I given the same answer to his sister, then age eleven, I probably would have heard, "Well, it depends on what you mean by *love*. Isn't it safe to say there are different kinds of love? And yes, while you may not be biologically related, marriage does seem to confer some type of connection, that while it might not be …"

"Randi, please get in here. Hannah has some questions for you."

Picture books—or as they are often called, "life books"—are a touching way to explain to little ones their personal story. My wife put together several of these for the children. Using drawings, stickers, photos and narrative, the books talked about a mommy and daddy who wanted a family, how God gives children in different ways, how special and loved this new child is, basically anything that would help illustrate the adoption journey from the beginning.

Initially Randi read these with the kids, but in time they picked them up themselves. Probably the books were one reason we heard less adoption curiosity than we expected. The personalized stories anticipated and addressed some of the kids' questions before they voiced them.

The composition of the books did evolve some over ten kids. The older kids' books were about a hundred pages, hardbound, with gilded printing and a foreword by Bill Cosby or Mother Teresa. The younger ones got three-by-five index cards with stick figures, two color crayon drawings and a one-sentence foreword written by an older sibling. OK, a little hyperbole. But you parents of a brood can relate.

Let's pull it together:

1. Don't fear the adoption talk or talks. Seldom are they uncomfortable for the kids, particularly the younger ones.
2. Let the children guide you. In the day-to-day flow of life, they will come up with questions and observations naturally leaning toward their adoption story. If they don't you can use common situations as your springboard to the subject.
3. Common sense is more valuable than psychological correctness. What to say and how to say it comes best from a deep familiarity with your child, not some generic psychological technique.
4. Your children know and love you. Their adoption stories will add to who they are but will not deny who their mom and dad are.

∴ ∴ ∴

THE REJECTION PERCEPTION

Dear Dr. Ray: I have a daughter, age six, adopted as a baby. She has lately asked what was wrong with her that her birth mom "gave her up." I don't want her thinking she was the reason.

—Accepting Mom

When I was a young shrink—a "shrinkling"—I studied a therapeutic system called rational emotive therapy (RET). Its main tenet asserts that our thoughts give rise to and shape our feelings. We continuously interpret what happens to us, forming conclusions that are sometimes reasonable and realistic and sometimes irrational and erroneous. To the extent that our perceptions about ourselves and others are inaccurate, we experience more self-defeating, negative emotions.

In fact, many counselors today practice some version of RET. It identifies a number of core misperceptions common to most people.

One, called "personalization," is the tendency to interpret others' behavior as a reflection upon ourselves. For instance, say you greet a coworker with "Good morning," and he doesn't acknowledge you. How quickly would you conclude that he must be upset with you? Or suppose your six-year-old daughter pilfers a little toy from her cousin's stash. Would you view this as a sign of some weakness in your parenting? Although other explanations could be possible in either situation, we tend to list ourselves as the first cause.

Everybody personalizes some. RET maintains that personalization is linked to human wiring, which means it begins very young. Even little kids personalize, though not so much as we grown-ups. (We've had a lot more years to practice it.) And despite how we parents try to teach otherwise, some bits and pieces of personalizing creep into the youngest personalities.

This phenomenon can afford you some comfort. That is, you needn't personalize your daughter's personalizing. It's highly unlikely it's your fault. You didn't do or not do anything to nurture her thought that something about her led her birth mom to "give her up." She is perfectly capable of misinterpreting her birth circumstances all by herself, thank you. There now, doesn't that make you feel better?

Couple the human proclivity to personalize with a situation puzzling to a little person, and you have the makings of a misperception. Fortunately, it's not generally an entrenched one. It should respond to a little correction and clarification by a big person. I only wish all therapy were so easy.

Recall the scenario involving my son Peter, at age five, asking, "Why didn't she keep me?" Recall also that one adult explanation sufficed to dispel his question. Peter was not unusual in his quick acceptance of the facts. He'd never thought of it Dad's way, and my way made sense, even if in part it was because Mom wasn't around to give him the real scoop.

Whatever explanation you offer your daughter, it's likely to reassure her. You may have to reiterate it every so often, but few little kids hold tight to their personalization in the face of a loving, logical parental interpretation. She sees you as semi-omniscient, as knowing the true story. When you offer it she'll probably feel both comfort and clarity.

So what might you say? Figuring out some psychologically savvy or profound formula isn't necessary. The goal is, in your own way, to convey a few key truths.

First is the unquestionable courage of her birth mom in making her decision. She gave your daughter birth to give her life. Hers was a profound act of love.

Second, her birth mom had to seek what was very best for her baby. She decided it would be to have a mom, dad and family. She couldn't do that in her life, so she looked for someone who could.

Third, adoption is not an act of rejection; it's an act of reception. Your daughter was not only a life received but also a life received into a family waiting and wanting to love her. Rather than being given away, she was sought. Rather than being unwanted, she was wanted desperately. Her birth mother made it all begin. Your explanation is aimed at turning your daughter's whole perception upside down.

Last, you said you don't want your daughter to think that something wrong with her led to the adoption. Your revelations are a good first step toward correcting her thinking. However, even if initially she's slow to see it the right way rather than her way, time should help bring everything into clearer focus. The longer she lives in a loving family, the more she'll understand that her birth mom's reasons were motivated by love.

Personally, I know of no children adopted at infancy who have persisted in the rejection perception through childhood into adulthood. When their family life is positive, this shapes their perceptions of their own beginnings as positive.

Do humans ever outgrow personalizing? Not really. We may resist it better as we realize we're prone to it. But even as I write this, I'm wondering if you'll like it or like me. Will you hear what I said, and will you accept it? Or does the fault lie in my sloppy, unclear manner of expressing my thoughts? Where's a psychologist when I need one?

:   :   :

LOOKING FOR REASSURANCE

Dear Dr. Ray: My nineteen-year-old adopted daughter has just told me she wants to find and meet her birth mom. She's talked about it some the past few years, but now she seems determined. I'm trying not to feel threatened by this.

—*Searching for Reasons*

We've talked the percentages. Despite widespread misperception, the actual number of adoptive children who seek birth parents is under 10 percent—though this statistic is not reassuring to you at the moment, as your daughter sounds to be in that 10 percent.

What's more, this statistic may actually cause you insecurity. That is, if it's uncommon for kids to search for birth roots, you may be wondering what is it about you or your family situation that led to this one-in-ten happening.

The question is not, "What is it about you?" The question is, "What is it about her?"

All throughout this book we talk from various angles about the wide inborn personality variability across kids. In that diversity most likely lies the answer to the real question. It could be that her sensitive nature, her emotionality, her social awareness, her tendency to question or some other factor is driving her desire to search.

For the most part our ten children reflect the statistical picture. Only a couple have voiced interest in their early past, even though five are now of legal age to act. One in particular is asking more questions than any of his siblings. As far as we can tell, he's been raised in the same family as all the others, by the same parents, with the same expectations and the same views of life. It appears his level of curiosity is unique to him. If it reflects something about us, both my wife and I are missing it. I can understand my being oblivious, but Randi? Highly unlikely.

One question ago I talked about the very human proclivity to personalize, to see ourselves as a cause for someone else's behavior, when in fact we're only a limited influence if at all. Personalizing gets stronger as we get older. While the littlest of little kids can personalize, adults are even more so inclined. Why?

Adults are more sophisticated than children in our thinking abilities. A young child is limited in forming conclusions—wrong or right—by the relative simplicity of his or her reasoning skills and perceptions. A grown-up is capable of a lot more speculation about a matter—some of it on the mark, some questionable, some downright mistaken.

Recall the suggestion I offered to the mom in the last question? It was to use her accurate adult assessment to correct her child's inaccurate one. Further, because her daughter trusted her mother, she would likely accept Mom's way of seeing things. In little people's eyes big people have big credibility. Until the little people get the eyes of teens, anyway.

You are not a little girl. For our purposes that means two things:

One, your reaction to your daughter's recent interest in her birth mom may be complex, as it is intertwined with your self-image as a mom. That little girl a few pages ago was linking few of her feelings with her status as a daughter. She simply had a question for which she had no answer.

Your self-perception is likely the context within which you interpret your daughter's birth interest. That is, you've always seen yourself as Mom, not a substitute, a stand-in or a parent double. Therefore it's natural for you to wonder if your status in your daughter's eyes has changed any, given her newly felt search urge.

Two, you are less likely, indeed probably less willing, than a young child to consider another's viewpoint on a problem. This is no criticism of your personality; it is a given of human existence. As we get older we are more inclined to see our way as the more realistic or better way. In other words, it takes more to persuade us to a different line of thinking.

If you were six and I were your father, I think I'd have a fair amount of influence with you. Thus, I could probably reassure you out of your personalizing. Since you're older, and at most I'm old enough to be your older brother, I'm left to rely on my psychology degree and adoptive fatherhood to convince you that your daughter's behavior is most likely little reflection on you. I hope that time will also confirm for you my perspective.

What about the practical question, should you offer to help her search? Some preliminary factors to consider are: Do you know who and where her birth mom is? Has there been ongoing contact, even if only between you and the birth mom? Do you have any way of knowing if she wishes to be located? Has she listed her name with the adoption registry available in some states? Does the agency, attorney or caseworker have any relevant information?

It's wise, however possible, to explore any such questions before acting. They can dramatically impact a reunion, for better or worse. If it's unclear whether the birth mom desires a connection or how one might be arranged, caution is the word. A birth mom's wishes for no contact need to be honored. At which point you'll have to focus your energy on helping your daughter assimilate the unexpected turn of events—what it means, whether it's temporary or permanent, what the birth mom's motives are, where you and your daughter go from here. In essence, you may have to help her depersonalize.

On the other hand, if the birth mom is eager for reunion, then barring exceptional circumstances, I would suggest you offer to help your daughter. Legally she is an adult. Wise or not, she has the option and right to make such a personal decision. Should you withhold your guidance, you put her in a loyalty bind. If she seeks her birth mom, she upsets Mom. If she acquiesces to

Mom's feelings, she turns her back on her birth mom. Better not to force her into such a dilemma, as she likely won't feel good about whatever path she takes.

Then too, by helping your daughter you show yourself to be Mom in the fullest sense of the word. You're not afraid or threatened by this other woman. Rather you too see her as someone meaningful to your daughter, not as someone to compete with for her affection. In essence, you reveal yourself to be quite mature about this whole affair.

Even if it's hard to feel good about what's unfolding, try to control any outward expression of hurt. Act as though you are settled inside. Put bluntly, fake it. In the first place, you won't have any regrets if the meeting turns out to be a one-time occurrence, and your daughter has to adjust to some disappointing realities. You didn't complicate the picture with your reactions. Second, your daughter will see you as understanding and supportive, willing to put your feelings second to hers. In communication language, you will have set up a win-win scenario.

Practically speaking, neither you, nor I, nor your daughter nor the birth mom, if located, knows how this will play out. Right now your daughter's determination is mainly an idea in her head. How that idea exactly will be made real is the major unknown. Will she find her birth mom? What will she find if she does? Will her birth mom be ever so pleased or ever so surprised? Will there be other family members, and what do they know about your daughter? What will be the nature of their relationship henceforward?

Put another way, whatever it looks like in your daughter's mind, the actual reunion may be warm or cool, a loving embrace or a shock. Her expectations may be fully, partially or minimally met. If things don't unfold as your daughter hopes, you—and your husband, of course—are the adults she'll be leaning on, as you always have been.

In the end your daughter will likely pull closer to you. You will be standing by, ready to share her joy or to pick up any emotional pieces. As you have done so many times in the years of her childhood, you will be there as Mom to help her through the consequences of her decisions. In so doing your status as Mom will only rise in her eyes.

: : :

A PARTLY OPEN BOOK

Dear Dr. Ray: My wife and I know a fair amount about our nine-year-old son's history, whom we adopted at age four, and it's messy. How much of it do we need to share with him?

—Too Aware

Before I answer your question, permit me to ask a few of my own. (We counselor types like to answer questions with questions—sometimes, I think, just to stall for time.)

As a teenager did you do some things that make you now cringe as you recall them? Was it conduct that would rattle you badly if done by your own children? Do you even today thank God for his help in navigating you past your own foolishness? Maybe more than once?

If you're anything like I am, your answers will be yes, yes and yes. Further, you don't and, I might add, shouldn't, tell your kids every incriminating detail of your wrongheaded past. They don't need to know. It isn't relevant to their present moral guidance. It most certainly isn't relevant to your present moral authority as a parent—no matter how much your kids fling at you, "You did this stuff when you were my age."

The parallels aren't perfect, but your past and your son's do share some common themes. First, how much does he really need to know about his early years? He's still a child, one hopes with some natural optimism and innocence left, even given what he might have seen or lived through. A prime benefit of a good present is that a bad past tends to fade from memory or at least loses some of its emotional grip.

Since you're not certain what your son knows or remembers, you risk supplying information that would be new to him, possibly upsetting. Whatever you know that he doesn't about his earlier life, you're far more able to put it in context than he is. Giving someone the total truth for the sake of full openness is not a good philosophy of life. Try telling a relative that you've noticed her gaining weight the past few years. Share with your spouse how negative you felt toward her before you calmed yourself down and realized you were wrong. Much in life is better left unsaid. That may include much that you know about your son's birth parents and their lives.

So do you say nothing? Act as if little took place in those years? Not necessarily. You can guide what you do say with a few questions. What is the purpose? Does your son need to know what you know? How will it help him—socially, emotionally, morally? What will it do to his image of his birth mom or dad? Will it needlessly tarnish it?

We adults may be greatly upset over what this little guy experienced. We may be struggling to suppress our own sense of tragedy at his treatment, but he doesn't need to feel the same sense. Again, why should he? A given of human nature is that kids are more resilient than grown-ups. Allow his youth to help him heal or forget or leave behind whatever happened.

What if a child knows little about the ugly in his past? He was adopted very young, and few memories formed. Good. His age insulated him.

"Watch your logic, Dr. Ray. My past is mine, so I can keep it to myself if I want. But the past we're considering is his. Shouldn't he know it if he wishes?"

Yes. If he were an adult as you are. Can we not assume you're better able to absorb and make sense of your history? As a child he may not be able to digest the truth he hears. It may only lead to more questions and insecurity, at too young an age.

There's a wonderful vignette in Corrie Ten Boom's book *The Hiding Place*, her story of courage and survival in a concentration camp during World War II. At age ten or so she asked her father one of those difficult questions about sexual sin. Her father didn't want her young mind to know about this yet, so he was silent. They were riding the train together, and at the stop he asked her to carry his suitcase for him, which was obviously too heavy for her to handle.

"It would be a pretty poor father who would ask his little girl to carry such a load," her father said. "It's the same way...with knowledge. Some knowledge is too heavy for children. When you are older and stronger you can bear it. For now you must trust me to carry it for you."[1]

You are carrying what might be too weighty for your son right now. You are not denying him a birthright nor hiding his life from him. You are exercising good judgment about what is or is not beneficial to him. That isn't a lack of honesty; it's a gift of protection.

What about your son's curiosity as he gets older? One principle of disclosure is to follow his lead. When the questions come up, answer them, with a couple principles in mind:

Don't supply every gory detail. Ask yourself, is this necessary for an honest answer to his question? If his birth mother had drug addictions, he doesn't need to know what drugs she used and for how long, what hospitalizations she endured and what were her legal troubles. He can get the straight truth with, "Your birth mother sometimes used drugs, and this made it a lot harder for her to care for you as she wanted to." And even if she may not have always wanted to care for him, giving the benefit of the doubt is a soft way to convey a hard truth.

Sometimes you are wise to plead a variant of the Fifth Amendment: "I don't know a whole lot about who took care of you back then." Perhaps you do know some, but it is still true you don't know a whole lot. Maybe that's good for you too.

: : :

The View From Now

Dear Dr. Ray: My son is eleven. We've talked about how and why we adopted him as a baby. He is now asking more questions about his birth parents, mostly his birth mom. How do we best respond? She had a troubled history as far as we know.

—*Looking Back*

Some children show little curiosity about their birth parents. It isn't that they're burying it; they truly aren't having much. Maybe later in life they will but not presently.

Other children are eager to know what can be known. They aren't necessarily trying to fill an identity void; they merely have some questions. Such differences in kids may not reflect any differences in how they're being raised. Call it instead the natural variation in humans, little or big.

Sometimes adoptive parents wonder what they might have done or not done to stimulate a child's interest in his biological parent. Did they miss something? Were they not open enough to subtle signs of interest? Much of the time the answers are no and no. Not everything a child expresses points to deep psychological material. Some kids are just more curious than others.

What you tell your son about his birth parents obviously depends first upon what you know. If you know little—maybe he was placed with an agency immediately at birth, and you adopted through the agency—you don't have much to tell, even if you wanted to tell it. On the other hand, perhaps you have a detailed history, full of really good things and really bad things, and you're wondering how to sift and sort through it for young ears.

No matter how much information you're privy to, a few basic principles can guide you. Principle one: Spare the ugly details. They are generally neither necessary nor enlightening. The most shocking history can be softened and still be accurate. "Well, your birth mom was very young and not really able to care for and raise a child."; "She had some problems in her own family, so she wanted you to be given to us."; "Your birth mom and dad did some things that caused them some trouble, and they couldn't take care of a baby."

While acknowledging that the birth mom or dad's life may have been troubled, the specifics, even if known, may not constitute "healthy disclosure." What purpose would it serve to recount a graphic past, especially if it has little relevance to the child's present? Full revelation is not always and everywhere a sound principle. It depends upon what is being revealed to whom and why.

What if your son pursues the specifics? "What kind of troubles did she have?"; "Why couldn't they take care of a baby?"; "Why wouldn't their families help them out?" Again, truth with gentle restraint: "I think the family had their own troubles." "She didn't have a steady job"—you don't have to delve into all the reasons why she didn't or couldn't hold a job.

Your discretion is not because your son has no right to know; it's because of his age. Someday the same questions will get more details, as a fifteen-year-old can better emotionally assimilate those details than a nine-year-old.

Principle two: Focus on the light and not on the darkness. Maybe the birth mom abused drugs and alcohol, with accompanying child neglect, thus prompting forced removal by Child Protective Services. It would still be true to say, "She was a young mommy who was struggling to get her own life straight, but she couldn't at that time, so you were taken from her. Then you lived with someone else for a little while until you became our son." Or, "She made some bad decisions, but she wanted you to have a good family." In all but the most extreme circumstances, there will be positives to provide your child about his birth parents and their lives or at least positive ways to explain the past.

With our own children, if the subject arises, where we can we stress the birth mom's act of love and sacrifice, not only in choosing adoption but also in choosing to continue her pregnancy. We are deeply grateful to those young mothers for giving life and family to each of our children, and the kids hear our gratitude. No matter how stormy a birth mom or dad's life up to and during the pregnancy, in the end most acted in favor of their children. We know that, and we make sure the kids do too.

Principle three: The past is not the present. In many cases what is now going on in a birth parent's life is unlike what was once going on. The most irresponsible young people can mature, straighten up, settle down. In narrating negatives from then, you could send your child the wrong message about now. I wouldn't want my kids' image of their dad to be shaped by who I was at nineteen. I would hope that I've matured, at least a few years. It's only right and fair not to leave a youngster with impressions formed by information possibly no longer true.

Is all this partial, gentle revelation a sugarcoating of reality? Not at all. What you share and tell is truth. But it's truth spoken with sensitivity for your child, while giving the benefit of the doubt to a birth parent. Both your child and the birth parent deserve as much.

:   :   :

WHO WANTS TO KNOW?

Dear Dr. Ray: We adopted our son at age twelve. He doesn't want us to tell anyone about his past, as he is very embarrassed by it. How do we decide what, if anything, to tell whom?

—*Guardian of History*

An older adopted youngster presents a very different picture from that of the child adopted in infancy. Not only is there far more history pre-adoption, but the child may be well aware of that history. He or she lived it, endured it, perhaps had to survive it. Likely your son has some strong feelings and opinions about his experiences, the people who formed them and what he wants known to others, including perhaps even his present parents.

Not all older adopted kids are protective of their past, but many are. As you observed, some are embarrassed by the upheaval, chaos or abuse. They see their past as a reflection on them, and they conclude that the less others know about it, the less bad they look. Because they're now living a more normal existence, they see no reason to recall less stable days. In a word, why?

Some children quite understandably are eager to move forward. They have a new life, a good family, and talking an ugly past to others will only keep it more alive than they want. In essence, they have a healthy, adapting focus on the now.

Honoring a child's wishes in these cases is not only sensitive parenting but also smart parenting. First of all, it fosters a sense of trust. The child learns to rest secure in his parents' word that they will protect his yesterday. Especially if a child's life was once marked by unreliable, untrustworthy adults, he needs to see that there are people he can count on, beginning with his mother and father.

Second, it's emotionally risky to include others too quickly in ticklish family situations. To illustrate, suppose you and your spouse recently experienced some marital discord. While still upset you shared your distress with a close friend. Shortly thereafter you and your spouse resolved the problem, with plenty of apologies and good will. You thus feel a whole lot warmer toward your spouse.

Your friend, however, didn't personally experience your change of heart. Even if you share that all is now better, his or her poor opinions could linger, based upon your previous venting. Put another way, your friend may need more time to recover his or her positive view of your spouse.

Similarly, what you tell others about your son's earlier life may predispose them negatively toward him or make them wary of him. What's more, initial impressions are slow to dissipate; they need a lot of contradicting input to fully go away. For you the unhealthiness of your son's past can recede in the context of your healthier present. Others don't have your relationship with him. Their view may be based, perhaps unfairly, on what they've heard rather than what they've seen. Far better to let them form opinions from your son's *now* rather than his *then*.

What about those who do need to know—teachers, physicians, counselors?

The operative phrase here is "need to know." Obviously, some of your son's past is going to impact his present—his development, academics, conduct. Quite possibly assorted specialists may be called upon for guidance. In the protective context of their professional relationship with your son, they will need to know details and specifics. But what if your son doesn't want them to know?

Here you may have to assert your judgment over your son's objections. Wherever more complete knowledge will help your son, a professional needs to know.

To begin, explain to him that only the professionals will know such things, no one else. Further, they only want to know those pieces of his past relevant to what is happening now. They will not scour his life for every nitty-gritty detail to satisfy personal curiosity.

Two, no professionals will in any way think less of him. They are very familiar with the kinds of things he's embarrassed by, as they have heard such many other times. Neither will they think he's weird, bad or stupid. Their opinion of him will not be shaped by what happened to him back when.

Three, what a teacher, doctor or counselor hears is for the sole benefit of your son. It will guide them to better solutions for whatever troubles are still affecting him. They need all the pieces of the puzzle to form the most accurate picture. If some critical facts are kept from them, they could form some wrong ideas about how best to help. Without their knowing whatever is vital, the very things that your son wants to leave behind could intrude into his new life.

In the final judgment the ones who need to know are the professionals who want to make his life better.

Once again, respect your son's wishes for privacy about his past. The only exceptions would be with those who, in their helping capacity, need to know what happened when. He must learn to trust their integrity and good intentions, even if you initially have to mandate that trust.

chapter seven

ADOPTION SELF-IMAGE:
MYTHS AND TRUTHS

Want to learn a whole lot of new things about yourself—good and bad? Want to dramatically alter your self-image—up or down? Want to grow emotionally? Be humbled? Feel vulnerable? Change perspectives? Become a parent.

We discover much about ourselves as life and our choices place us in new situations. What we discover sometimes pleases us; sometimes it distresses us. Either way, if we're willing we can mature and alter our expectations to better fit reality.

Like all parents, adoptive parents learn much about themselves and their kids with time. They come face-to-face with certain realities. In the long run that is beneficial, no matter how disturbing it is initially.

: : :

IS LOVE ENOUGH?

Dear Dr. Ray,

We adopted twin girls, age six, two years ago. Both my husband and I thought that if we just loved them, they would thrive. It hasn't been that simple.

—*Loving Hard, But...*

Love is at the critical center of parenthood. Without it not much else good happens. Properly understood, love is more than critical; it is enough. The key, though, lies in what we understand love to be.

Most people think of love primarily as a blend of emotions: empathy, affection, kindness—you know, warm stuff. It is that, but it is much more. It is also commitment, perseverance, sacrifice and discipline.

Love in all its fullness will help your daughters thrive. Love as feelings and their expression, however positive, may indeed fall short in helping you raise well-adjusted children.

Many people who adopt older children see the pre-adoptive history as lacking in or devoid of emotional connections. Understandably they want to replace what was missing quickly and fully. The reasoning is: This child didn't have much love. I have plenty of love to give. If I restore the balance, the child will blossom. This sounds like your hope for your girls.

No doubt some kids do need extra hefty doses of acceptance and warmth immediately from their new parents in order to begin feeling secure. Such "warm love" can work magic in softening a sclerotic history. It may be, though, that the healing will take longer than you anticipated. Further, your love will need expression in ways that don't seem like love, at least at first look.

In addition to lots of affection, you will need lots of perseverance in teaching social skills. With all your encouragement will also come strong limits, especially on the girls' more resistant misconduct. Along with the family good times will be some "bad" times of asserting your authority.

Most of us readily recognize love shown through affection. It's much harder to sense the love in making a youngster stand in the corner or go to bed early because of a tantrum. As one mother told me, "Discipline is love in action," though it doesn't feel like love. It feels more like frustration, anger or distress—negative reactions at odds with love.

A critical point: Discipline itself is not mean or negative, though some people might approach it that way. Nasty words or verbal attacks certainly are unnecessary, even hurtful, and they are not discipline. They are emotional clutter that is counterproductive to good discipline.

It is not momentary feelings, positive or negative, that are at the defining core of love. It is commitment. It is love to supervise closely whom your girls associate with—for the next twelve years. It is love to scrutinize and monitor all the media seeking your daughters' attention, even if far more than do most American parents. It is love to give social freedom more slowly than others in their peer group get it. It is love to limit the trinkets and material goodies that might pour in from relatives, because you think they're too much for your children's good.

Despite whatever emotions accompany it, the purpose of such discipline is good. It is to teach and shape character. Indeed, if not for the underlying love motivating it, discipline alone would be too much of an unpleasant effort to continue for nearly two decades.

Love has many faces: softness, firmness, compromise, resolve, kisses, consequences. Some of those faces may look less like love than others, but all are still love. If that's the breadth of love you and your husband are talking about, then it is enough. And it is love that will help your girls thrive in your home and beyond.

∶ ∶ ∶

THE HALLMARK OF A GOOD FAMILY

Dear Dr. Ray: Our son is six. We adopted him at birth. I've tried so hard to make raising him positive and pleasant, but it's been frustrating. I think I was expecting a Hallmark card family.

—*June Cleaver*

Yours is a common adoption dynamic. Here's how it typically unfolds: A couple looking forward to having children finds they can't conceive. Pursuing adoption, they are apprehensive about when or if parenthood will happen. Eventually their dreams of a family are realized, as they adopt their first son or daughter. They are now determined to make family a warm, unquestionably positive experience for everyone. Their gratitude and excitement will be manifest in one of the most harmonious homes in recorded history, or at least in the Western Hemisphere this century.

In time this idyllic image runs headfirst into a formidable presence: the child. Mom and Dad may have anticipated peak family bliss, but somebody forgot to enlighten the youngster. Lacking any preconceived notions, he was primed to do what comes naturally—be a kid, with all the immaturity, impulsiveness, contrariness, unpredictability and willfulness that's part of the kid nature.

How and why your son might be dog-earing the edges of your Hallmark card, we discuss elsewhere in this book (see, for example, "The Relatability Factor" in this chapter), so I won't talk much more about him. Our focus here will be on you.

No doubt you eagerly anticipated being a mother—a really good one at that. You had loads of love and other gifts just looking for a recipient—in addition to your husband, of course. Perhaps you thought, as do many, that with enough love, affection and reason, your motherhood would be one rewarding experience after another. After all, if you treat your child warmly and well, he'll reciprocate.

Should a child's personality be so predisposed, some parents do live in such harmony all the way to the child's adulthood. Their early hopes are crystallized by their daily routine. Most kids, however, don't allow Mom and Dad to live out expectations that are too unrealistic.

It is not because the children are unruly; it's because they're normal, and they need hefty doses of both positive and "negative," that is, discipline, to learn to be positive, pleasant kids. To the extent any parents, natural or adopted, expect all positive with little negative, they will be disappointed, even self-doubting.

Let's use the bad news–good news dichotomy. The bad news is that you're not living exactly what you'd wished. You're discovering that, try as you might to set up win-win child-parent scenarios, your son is regularly driven toward one outcome: He wins. Consequently there are more contests, perhaps conflicts, than you think should be found in a Courier and Ives image.

Don't despair, you're just experiencing the standard stuff of child raising. Besides, I've wondered if Courier and Ives had any kids. If they did, one would expect to see at least a few crayon marks on their prints.

More bad news. You may have to reassess your style. Are you prepared to discipline more, with more resolve and more perseverance? If your son is getting progressively more uncooperative, it may not be because you're not positive enough. It could be because you're not firm enough.

"But how do I get firmer?"

I've written a number of books almost exclusively about discipline.[1] The techniques and principles in them are relevant to all children, preschooler to teen, adopted and biological. I refer you there rather than talking too far afield from the intent of this book. (How's that for a cheap, self-promoting sales pitch?)

Finally to the good news. And there's more of it.

First, you aren't being forced to abandon your desire for a highly rewarding family life. Not at all. You're accepting a truth: Great families begin with loving as well as strong parents. Your hopes weren't false; they were just being thwarted because you had some faulty notions about what raising your son would be like. Get rid of them—not your son—and you will better pursue your ideal of motherhood.

Second, kids are much more cooperative when they know your parameters. On one hand, maybe your son is the kind of child who smiles sweetly, acquiescing instantly to, "OK, Knap, we must ready ourselves for bedtime now. Did you add sticker number 40 to your chart? You know, this is your fortieth night in a row to bed on time without a fuss." Then you don't need discipline resolve. Just bask in your success, relishing the teeth-clenched envy of all us other parents.

On the other hand, if your son is human and resists a rest (sorry), then you're forced to act. "Knap, if you get out of bed, you'll lose all your stuffed animals and won't be allowed outside tomorrow." Wherein a fit may commence, you'll have to discipline again, and once more you'll have to quell your agitation over "Why can't this go more smoothly?" It could, if a child weren't involved.

The best news is last. With a healthy combination of love and discipline, you will likely achieve the heartwarming image of family you once looked toward. You may take a less direct path there, with some bumps you didn't foresee, but you'll still arrive. And you'll be less frustrated along the way, because your expectations will be much more in line with reality.

Now go get yourself another Hallmark card.

:   :   :

I'M REALLY GOOD, OR I WAS

Dear Dr. Ray: We have one biological daughter, age eight. Four years ago we adopted our second daughter at birth. She is more difficult to raise. With our first child I felt like a good parent. Now I'm having real doubts.

—Humbled

If it'll make you feel better, what you're experiencing is not unique to adoption. It's common with biological offspring. I've labeled it the "shell-shocked second child syndrome." Here's the pattern:

Child number one by temperament is cooperative, or mature, or thoughtful, or kind, or loyal and true blue or all of the above and then some. Put simply, the child is a delight. This has two effects.

One, the parenting journey is smooth. Little Lovina's persona is one of, "Oh, yes, Mother, I most certainly will do as you ask, because you are my mother, whom I love desperately, and because I fully recognize the wisdom in following your guidance." This is the kind of kid you trot out in public whenever possible in order to provide an example to other mere mortal parents.

The second effect of raising a Chastity or an Oxford: It makes you cocky. "I don't understand why all these people struggle. I must have the God-given instincts to raise bunches of children of any age. Other parents tell me of their discipline troubles, but I personally have never lived through that in my home. I guess some of us are just child-rearing naturals."

Sometimes a second child of easy temperament comes along, only more solidly locking in the conclusion that "this child-raising thing isn't so tough." After all, one great kid might be fortuitous chance, but two?

Routinely I ask parents who are flummoxed over disciplining a child, "Is there an older sibling?" Half as routinely I hear something like, "Oh, yes, and nothing at all like this. Our first child was normal. Any discipline troubles were few and short-lived. We talked, and she listened. Our first child was far more cooperative than this one is."

I follow up with, "What makes you think your first child was 'normal'? It sounds as if your second child is the normal one. Your first was a freebie, a mulligan round from God. He basically said, 'Here, practice on this one. I'll save the real kid for later.'"

Some kids have more potential to stretch our parenting to its limits. Whether strong willed or high maintenance or "a difficult child" (I think the term redundant) is often hard to know. What can be known is that this child is tougher than the older sibling, or siblings, to raise. That doesn't tell much about how easy the siblings might be, and that can confuse the whole family picture.

All this said, the fact is that your daughter lowers your self-image as a mother. Let's try to raise it some.

How are you a poorer mom because your daughter behaves in ways her sister doesn't? Much of what she does is no reflection on you; it's a reflection on her. Her conduct may be exasperating, relentless or slow to conform, but that doesn't mean you caused it. You have to respond to it, but much of its origin lies within your daughter. While this can lead to exasperation, it shouldn't lead to self-deprecation.

You may also have to broaden your perception of parenthood. Until four years ago your idea of mothering was largely shaped by your experience with your first child. It was accurate as far as it went. And it was pleasant. Now it is being formed further by a second experience, a more complex one. Both are legitimate. The second is very different from what you'd grown accustomed to and, might we say, preferred. This new parenting journey may have more agitation; that doesn't mean you're a poorer parent.

I am not seeking excuses for you nor downplaying your very real frustrations with your adopted daughter. I am pointing out the reality—for all parents—that some kids make us question ourselves more than others. Some are good at bringing out our bad habits. Some make us wonder how suited we are for this parenting thing.

Does this mean you'd best be prepared to live with some self-doubt? Perhaps, in the sense that any challenging child—naturally so or by comparison to a sibling—will evoke self-scrutiny. Did I handle that right? Am I being too permissive? Too demanding? Am I playing favorites? Does she notice my clenched teeth? My locked jaw? Such questions can be disconcerting; they don't have to be paralyzing. Self-doubt does its damage if we stay mired in it.

If you can weather her, a tougher kid can make you a better parent. How? By promoting self-scrutiny, which leads to self-awareness, which leads to self-improvement. How can I be calmer? Am I vigilant enough for this child's level of impulsiveness? Do I need to talk less and act more when it's time to discipline? Can I find new ways to compliment, pay attention, show affection? If self-doubt doesn't become a downward spiral, it can be a springboard to the kinds of questions we all need to ask anyway.

Look on the bright side. Without your second child you would most likely have continued believing you were superior to the rest of us. A comforting illusion, to be sure, but fragile in the face of kid reality. Your younger daughter will make you not only a more skilled mom but a humbler one. All in all, a great combination, especially if you decide to adopt again.

: : :

THE RELATABILITY FACTOR

Dear Dr. Ray: Six years ago we adopted Andrew, then age fourteen months, from overseas. We also have a biological daughter, age ten, and another adopted son, age four. I have to confess that I have trouble relating to Andrew. He is different from the other two in many ways.

—*Guilty Feeling*

Assume for the moment that your three children were triplets, identical in age, sex, genetics, nearly so in appearance. Even at that, none would be the same in personality. Thus, none would be the exact same to raise.

At the core of parenthood is an immutable truth: Every child is a unique experience. One will grab your hand and walk smiling at you each step of the way. Another will try to slap, even bite your hand, to escape and mark his own path. A third will journey with you some of the time, depending upon just where you're headed. I'm sure you know this. Parents, if not prepared early for all the variety in kids, are forced eventually by the kids themselves to realize and accept it.

Most parents adjust fairly smoothly to these natural differences, as long as they're not too marked. Distress can arise when one child is radically unlike any siblings, however so—in emotional makeup, social sense, affection, response to discipline. Because of who he is, a child can evoke the beauty in a parent or sometimes the beast. Her emotions can fuel our emotions. His reaction to discipline can shape our discipline. Her impulsiveness can shorten our patience. His lack of affection can cool our affection.

Put another way, who a child is influences, for good or ill, who we are. What's more, who we are with this child may not please us. We understandably don't like feeling unfair, moody, distant or edgy. And we wonder how much the child notices.

To be sure, your son is quite unlike your other children to raise. You've concluded so after six years of living with him. The question you've no doubt pondered for six years is *why?* As said above, the most straightforward answer is: He is who he is. To which you've also wondered, "Why is he who he is?" Is it inherited from birth parents? Is it the fourteen months of life before us? Is it something about the adoption? Is it something about me? Is it all of the above?

To help answer these questions, ask yourself a few: First, what do you know about your son? Why was his birth mom unable or unwilling to raise him? Was it because of her circumstances? Emotional fragility? Personality struggles? Which of these could be genetically passed on, at least in part?

Was your son's womb environment healthy? Free of drugs and alcohol? Nutritionally sound? Stress-free? What level of medical care was there—for baby and mother?

Where and how were your son's first fourteen months spent? With whom? If in an institutional setting, was there neglect? How much human interaction was there? Stimulation? Language formation?

You likely have only incomplete answers to some or most of these questions. But you know that your son did not begin his life with all the advantages you could have given him—meaning, whatever was lacking or questionable from his conception forward might now be impacting his development. Even if nothing obvious—physical, medical or intellectual—is present, there may be little subtleties in his makeup that affect his maturity, judgment, impulsiveness or sociability.

What might his past portend for the present? Several things.

One, your son's personality may show some rough edges. This is not to say that eventually he won't grow up as you hope. It says that the journey could be characterized by more zigs and zags, by two steps forward and one back. While your other kids, for instance, abandoned temper flares after three months of good discipline, this little guy may need three years merely to tone down his decibel level to 110. Understanding the reality can reduce frustration when you have to live with it, and live with it, and live with it and ...

Two, as I've said other places, your feelings are not the defining characteristic of your motherhood. Your motherhood at its heart is founded upon your commitment to your son. "For better or worse" is central not only to marriage but also to the parent-child bond. You always love your son, though at times you may not "feel" so. Even as you feel guilty at not always experiencing the level of warmth for your son that you'd like, be reassured that you are still persevering in the staples of parenthood—sacrifice, discipline, supervision.

Emotions come and go; commitment remains. Never lose the long-term focus. You are committed to being Andrew's mother, no matter how much he stresses your commitment along the way.

"But I don't like feeling unmotherly toward my son." Quite understandable. There are no magic words to quickly soothe your emotions. Still, with time and honest effort, your feelings should become less volatile. Your reactions will become more tempered. In essence, your commitment to your son will soften your exasperation.

Point number three: You love all your children equally; it doesn't follow that you can relate equally easily to all of them. Call it the relatability factor. You don't relate with the same ease to all the grown-ups in your life; why would you expect to do so with children? Some kids' personalities or styles are just better fits to our own. This in no way means you love your children unequally. It means you might interact with them differently—and that's all right.

"But I don't want to act differently with the kids. I want to treat them all the same."

How is that possible? They don't all act the same. So at some level your treatment of each will be distinct. Each child will make it so, whether you wish it or not.

However, you can still strive—all the rest of your parenthood—not to overreact to the more maddening child. Parents get frustrated. We don't have to act as frustrated as we feel.

Over the years keeping my cool with some of my children has taken more effort than with others. This isn't a sign of favoritism;

it's a given of human interaction. I've also learned that this parenting "weakness" can make me a stronger parent. Meaning, how hard is it to stay sweet and calm with a child who is sweet and calm? It takes a lot more parental resolve, not to mention maturity, to stay sweet and calm—OK, maybe just calm—with the child who has little interest in bringing out such characteristics in me.

A great benefit to being in the family-and-kid business for nearly thirty years is being able to observe firsthand some long-term trends. One of the more encouraging is what I call "the tough kid paradox." More than a few veteran parents who initially sought my help with their most recalcitrant youngster have later told me what an admirable young adult the child has become. It took years, but the ending for the whole family was pretty happily ever after.

: : :

The Name Is Bond

Dear Dr. Ray: We adopted our son two years ago at age five. I've read a lot about a child struggling to bond with a parent. What about a parent—me—struggling to bond with the child?
—*Sticking With It*

We'd better define *bond* before we define *struggling*. Simply, *bond* means to emotionally attach. As a noun *bond* is the connection between child and parent grounded upon love and commitment.

Talk to a hundred adoption professionals, and you could get a hundred variations on the bonding theme. Here you'll get my understanding of what has become a catchword in the adoption lexicon, for better or worse.

Bonding most often is analyzed from a child's perspective. Because any relationship by definition involves at least two people, bonding also can be a grown-up problem. Bonding struggles can go both ways.

Typically when an adoptive parent confesses a struggle similar to yours, underneath it is the questions, "Is this somehow related to the adoption?" More exactly, "If the child were mine by biology, would I feel differently?" And, "Are my feelings a sign of some character deficit in me?"

Some heavy stuff here—enough to shake up even a once stable parental self-image. Let's try to restabilize.

Bonding distress is usually voiced by parents who have adopted older children. Infant adoptions offer a period of attachment simpler than that with an older child. Infants do show unique temperaments—some easy, some tough. Nevertheless, the relationship between caretaker and child starts to solidify from day one. It continues through a few years of interaction on nurturing terms—holding, cuddling, feeding, needs expressed and needs met—God's design for forming a bond.

An older child presents a more defined identity. He or she enters the family with a personality already somewhat shaped. Both the child and the adult must learn to relate to and get along with each other soon. There is no infant cuddly period or year of natural connecting. The child is a little person, not a baby anymore, capable of bringing out both the pretty and the ugly in a big person.

As I emphasize in several other places, some kids—by nature, by turbulent history or by both—present child-rearing challenges over and above the norm. If your child is one of these, forging a solid emotional tie could take some time. Don't think that you're not embracing parenthood. Realize that you're finding the embrace to require more perseverance than you originally thought it would.

A good counselor seeks to help the client discern accurately what is going on inside. It's easy to be confused about one's emotions and to call them something they're not. Could your parenting struggles be more related to frustration than bonding? Would you feel more warmth if you weren't so regularly agitated? It's hard for soft feelings to grow in the soil of exasperation. Perhaps your lack of bonding would be more accurately labeled an excess of frustration.

Am I playing with words? No matter what one calls it—weak bonding or strong frustration—isn't the reality the same? Yes and no.

Yes, the experience is the same, that is, "I don't feel as parental as I think I should." No, in that "weak bond" carries much heavier implications. It connotes weak affection, possibly weak love. What parent wants to think this about himself? Therefore, it's wise to make sure it's true before believing it.

A struggle to bond is often a struggle to relate to a child because of aloofness, deceptiveness, contrariness, explosiveness—from the child, that is, though any of that can evoke some of the same from us. Mom or Dad isn't necessarily a failure in the emotional stuff of parenthood; it may be that the early rockiness of the parent-child relationship is stunting the growth of warmth.

To be blunt, don't be too ready to conclude you're not bonding. As long as you continue to show the good things of motherhood—commitment, sacrifice, guidance—and don't deliberately withdraw emotionally, time is your ally. Eventually the bond you worried wasn't coming will begin to grow in the emotional dimensions you seek.

What if your son senses your inner turmoil—be it frustration or slow bonding? Take some advice from the ancient philosophers: Act good even if you feel bad. Show affection when you might not want to. Compliment though the words are sticking in your throat. Speak calmly even as you want to scream the roof off. Kiss good night when you'd rather wave. If you don't feel connected, act as if you do.

Feelings often follow conduct. Your good actions will bring out good feelings from both your son and you, fostering a genuine bond.

One final consolation: If negative emotions stay internal, they're much harder for another to sense. Others, particularly little others, see outward actions as revealing inward inclinations. That is, your son will conclude that your positive behavior is a sign of your positive emotions toward him. I doubt he'll think, "Sure. You're nice to me. But that's only because you really don't like me," unless he happens to be one overanalyzing, complex kid—or a shrink.

chapter eight

ADOPTION DISCIPLINE BASICS

Adoptive parents routinely wonder if disciplining an adoptive child is different from disciplining a biological child. Indeed, I've been asked, "When are you going to write a book on discipline for adoptive parents?" To which I reply, "I already have. My discipline books are for any kind of parent with any kind of kid."

The basics of discipline—rationale, expectations, limits backed by consequences—are pretty much similar for all children. And that's good news for all parents. It's effort enough getting good at everyday discipline without having to master another set of principles for "special" circumstances.

Nonetheless, adoptive parents do confront some discipline questions particular to them. A few such questions follow. The answers don't require new discipline directions, just learning what temptations to resist and what realities to recognize.

: : :

MISGUIDED COMPENSATION

Dear Dr. Ray: I have two adopted children, ages nine and four, from overseas. They were neglected as infants. Sometimes it's hard for me to discipline them because of that. I feel guilty.

—*Tentative*

Some twenty years ago I wrote a book titled *You're a Better Parent Than You Think!* (Yes, I was the only freshman in my high school to author a book.) In it was a chapter titled "How to Talk Yourself out of Authority," which contained a section called "Balancing the Scale, or He's a Special Child." I think what I wrote then might have some relevance for you. Permit me to quote myself:

> One of the fixed conditions of our existence is that life is not fair. (I was quite profound in those days.) It does not treat people with the same degree of kindness, not even the most innocent and helpless among us....
>
> Because you feel her pain when a child seems to be a victim of a capricious and often callous world, you want very much to find some way to make things up to her, to turn her world into a nicer place.... But in your desire to compensate for the injustices done your child, it's quite easy to go too far, to do the one thing that can undo much of the good you've gained by everything else: You can deny yourself the right to put limits and expectations upon your youngster's behavior....
>
> ...With a special child, a suspension of discipline may be well intentioned, but it is misguided. It will not make

amends for an unjust world; it will only create more injustice —for you, immediately; for your child, with time. She will form distorted expectations of life…. She will learn from painful experience that her special condition, which some may not even consider to be special, carries no license to treat others shabbily or command special allowances for her behavior. Ultimately, in addition to not righting the scale, forfeiting your authority may bring about the very same result you wanted to avoid in the first place. Instead of making your youngster more emotionally durable, … she will probably become even less so, as she grows accustomed to obstacles always being removed.[1]

How much you avoid discipline because of guilt or a desire to compensate I don't know. But I do know that no matter what your kids experienced back then, you don't give them a better now by being permissive. Compensate in other ways—find more time to talk, make a little more space on your shoulder to cry on, reach deeper inside yourself to feel what they feel. Do not, however, neglect discipline. Your children already have had one form of neglect; best not to add another.

Parents who adopt older kids often wrestle with two opposing tendencies. On one hand they feel sorry for their children because of their early histories; thus such parents become tentative in their authority. On the other hand, because these children need hefty doses of strong parenting to make up for socialization lost, the parents get frustrated with how slowly things progress. The outcome is loss of confidence with gain of guilt.

You must deal with your children's behavior in the present. What they endured some years ago may be related to today, but you can't know how any more than vaguely. Defiance is still defiance, whether its roots were laid down six years ago or yesterday. For your child's sake you must answer it firmly, even if all the while you fight guilt.

Believe it or not, you can feel guilty and still act resolutely. It takes a little practice. Fortunately, children give us lots of opportunities to practice resolute discipline despite our internal state.

Good discipline is often a matter of mind over heart. Here's a thought for your mind during discipline times: You are the most loving, softest teacher about life your children will ever have. If you don't discipline today, for whatever reason—guilt, compensation, fear of psychological incorrectness, laziness—the world will tomorrow. All children will be disciplined. The question is, *by whom?*

Discipline without love may be harsh; love without discipline is child abuse. Ultimately an undisciplined child will get hurt by a world that reacts adversely to undisciplined people, by a world that doesn't allow too many mitigating circumstances. No police officer, employer or judge is likely to say, "Oh my, you have identity problems, you're left-handed, and you were adopted from overseas? I'm glad I know that. It changes everything."

Even your firmest, strictest discipline impulses are gentler than those of the world. Your discipline comes with soft landings. The world's doesn't.

Don't let your children's questionable beginnings inhibit your discipline by creating needless guilt. Yes, it is tempting to go easier on them now because life was harder on them before. But if you yield to the temptation, you will only hurry along the day that your kids will be disciplined by another. And that day will be longer and harder on them than you would have ever been.

Equal Treatment

Dear Dr. Ray: Simple question: Do I discipline my adopted son (age five) differently than I do my birth son (age nine)?

—Disciplinarian Dad

Simple answer: No. But since I am a shrink, I can't leave it at that.

Obviously you discipline according to the nature of the child. Each child's innate personality will require more or less, milder or firmer discipline. No two kids, even identical twins, ask of parents identical discipline.

That's not exactly what you asked though. It seems you were asking, "Does adoption itself, and whatever issues might surround it, lead to a different discipline approach?" Again I'll say no. But again, I can't leave it at that.

Whether or not your adopted son presents you with a personality, history or development radically unlike his brother's is only slightly relevant to your discipline. Yes, you may need more sensitivity to whatever might be unique to him and his conduct, but discipline is still discipline.

If big brother pushes little brother, will he not, say, have to spend time in the corner? If little brother pushes older brother, will there be less corner time or fewer sentences to write or a smaller loss of privileges? Possibly, because of his age, but not because of his status. A kid is a kid, and discipline is discipline.

Maybe your adopted son will need sixty-seven corner visits as opposed to his brother's twenty-one to learn to keep his hands to himself. Still, the essence of the discipline is the same for both boys: You do *x, y* happens.

Several months after we adopted Jonathan and Joanna at age four, they were still getting more discipline than our other four children (ages six to one). One night, after a particularly exasperating series of misbehavior from Jon, I lamented to my wife, "Maybe we should drop our standards with the twins, so the discipline isn't so lopsided. We can ratchet up our expectations again as the kids come to learn better self-control."

My wife, blessed naturally with more parental wisdom than I, said, "You big dummy. What are you talking about?"

OK, she didn't actually say that, but given her pause before she spoke, I was wondering for a few seconds if that's what she was thinking. She really said, "Ray, how do we do that? Do the other children get into trouble for throwing a fit, but Jon and Jo don't, unless they get really carried away? Do we make the others stay in bed at bedtime, but Jon and Joanna can get up if they want? Just how do we have separate sets of rules, and how will the kids perceive that?"

In defense of myself, I did realize quickly she was right. Trying to orchestrate two distinct sets of discipline rules across kids would lead to heavy confusion for everybody. Our standards had to be house standards for all.

We did, however, give Jon and Jo extra hugs, kisses and attention to counterbalance their getting more consequences than the others. I'd highly recommend doing this with any kid on the receiving end of more than the average amount of discipline. Make sure you give heavy doses of positives to help offset what could seem negatives to the child. All Spike knows is that he gets into the most trouble. He is not likely to attribute it to his conduct but rather to your "unfairness." Alas, such is the nature of kids, big people too.

Another suggestion: Practice staying calm. Having to discipline one child more than another, or more than all the others together, especially if the difference is major, can get very frustrating. Over time this can show itself ever more obviously. Therefore, work to convey more resolve than volume. You'll gain credibility and kindness by telling Angel firmly, "Please go to your room," rather than by ranting at 110 decibels why she'd better be sitting on her bed within the next four seconds or else. Both are expressions of discipline; one is meaner about it.

Often it is the harshness or the tone or the emotion, and not the discipline, that makes a child feel as though he's the favorite discipline target. Suppose Oxford has to cool on the couch six times a day while Brother sits once every six days. Oxford will likely sense less inequity if he also senses less parental distress over how he acts. In other words, it's the frustration and not the discipline that sends the negative message.

To pull it together, the expectations of discipline are fairly identical across kids, natural or adopted. The rules are similar, the limits are similar, even the consequences are similar. It is the enforcement—when, how often and how firmly—that can vary noticeably from child to child. Further, while nondiscipline factors can affect the whole discipline picture, these are best dealt with directly and not through altering one's standards.

So did our twins' rate of discipline ever slow to that of the other kids? Somewhat. Over a few years they gradually internalized better behavior. As I look back from here, though, I believe the real remedy kicked in when we adopted a couple more little ones needing even more discipline than Jon and Jo. By comparison they saw themselves as poster children for "Discipline Today." Talk about the power of a changed self-perception.

:　:　:

LOOKING FOR GREENER GRASS

Dear Dr. Ray: My fifteen-year-old adopted son has begun saying, "I want to find my birth mom," when we make a discipline decision he finds disagreeable. What do I say to that, if anything?

—*Slow to Respond*

When kids disagree with discipline or rules or limits, they don't typically retort with, "Mother, while I recognize that in your own misguided way you are striving to teach me morals and character, I must register my dismay and frustration over your present parenting course." If they did, they probably wouldn't have needed much discipline in the first place. Or they would need to be referred to some university center for unearthly phenomenon.

No, when kids disagree with discipline, they routinely fire off verbal salvos unrelated to the discipline itself but laser-guided at our soft spots, sometimes even our jugular. Thus, "I don't like you," or "I'm running away," or "I wish Grandma were my mom; she loves me" or "I wish Dad were my mom; he's not home much" can all be little-kid comebacks to your yucky parenting moves.

Getting bigger means getting better at pinching sensitive nerves. Older kids can voice more hard-hitting opinions.

"When I'm eighteen, I'm out of here." Despite its teen popularity, this one's not a real threat—hope?—for the majority of parents. Given most kids' level of material comfort, they're far less likely than their predecessors to grab independence as soon as legally able. After all, how many can afford a ninety-eight-inch-screen TV, complete with surround sound and 1,257 channels in their first week of heavenly freedom?

Not uncommonly a teen will fling at his single parent that he's ready to live with the other parent if things don't improve (read "get more permissive") at home. Some kids even threaten to sic the authorities on their parents—for no reason other than that they're being strong parents.

It's not inconceivable then that an adoptive child may vocalize a desire to seek his roots upon momentarily deciding things aren't exactly to his liking at Mom and Dad's place. These expressions—regardless of how creative or designed to hurt—are wrapped around one theme: "It's so bad here that any grass anywhere else would be greener." Fortunately, most such commentary is fleeting and doesn't reflect a pervasive attitude.

Certainly adoptees have many reasons for curiosity about their birth parents, mostly unrelated to discipline disgruntlement. Yet some, during an emotional surge, do imagine another world out there more "understanding" than their current one, and they'd like to find it.

Your question makes it sound as though your son is in this latter group, considering the fact that he only voices birth parent curiosity at discipline time. That doesn't mean he never thinks about his roots otherwise; it means that his interest flares up at predictable times. Because kids can have an honest interest about something doesn't mean they won't ever use it as a manipulation tool.

I would acknowledge your son's comeback but not act on it. For example, "Well, when you're eighteen, and if you still want to seek out a birth parent, we can talk. Until then this isn't something we can pursue." Or, "It sounds like you're upset because I'm not acting as you think I should."

Is there a risk of minimizing or ignoring some real issues for your son? A better question is, how real are they? You know your son better than anyone, and you've judged that his words are aimed at you and don't reflect an irresistible attraction to else-where. Therefore, respond to what is actually bothering him if you see best, but don't feel obliged to explore what he wants you to think is bothering him.

It is true that for a child—even one fifteen years old—actively searching for a birth parent, except in most unusual circum-stances, is not an option. In today's computer-linked world, he may try to seek identifying information, but the real-life search cannot generally be pursued. Maybe it will be someday, but not today.

Further, is discipline disgruntlement always something that needs your urgent attention? Would you sit down and discuss in depth with your six-year-old why he wants to run away anytime he's denied an open bedtime? Would you arrange a "time to talk" whenever your sixteen-year-old promises to move out at age eighteen? Well, OK, maybe you would be tempted to reserve an apartment in case she has a change of heart by the following week.

Get a kid upset enough over your parenting, and he could reach for about anything to say. Your son may believe what he is saying while he's still mad, but that doesn't mean he truly means what he is saying. Emotions spur a lot of unmeant words—for kids and adults. The key to being a savvy parent is to know when to look for the meaning in words and when not, when to react to them and when not.

: : :

Totally RAD

Dear Dr. Ray: Two families in our adoption support group have shared that their children show signs of "reactive attachment disorder" (RAD). I've read about this, but I'm still not really clear on what it is.

—*Overreacting*

Some of your confusion may be due to the looseness of the "symptoms" popularly attached to the diagnosis. According to a number of articles, these include—but are not limited to—pushing love away, inappropriate affection with strangers, lack of affection in response to parents, being superficially charming with others, poor peer relationships, lack of self-control at home, emotional phoniness, lack of eye contact with adults, resistance to physical closeness, clinging behavior, avoidant behavior, persistent chatter, lack of conscience, lack of impulse control, poor understanding of cause and effect, manipulation, inner anger, anxiety, inability to accept no, turning everything into a battle, lying, stealing, self-destructive or accident-prone behavior, eating disorders, cruelty to animals.

Are things clearer now?

The list is only a small sampling of what I have read. It could be expanded, as more signs of reactive attachment disorder have been cited by other adoption professionals. Still it paints the picture. RAD—you know something is well known when it's recognized by its initials—has grown maddeningly diffuse in its boundaries. What's more, notice how it coincides with much problem behavior that can be rooted in other causes.

With the exception of the more serious stuff (such as cruelty to animals, stealing, lack of conscience, eating disorders), it would seem many kids more or less exhibit some of these "signs" intertwined with normal development. They are connected with the whole process of maturing—learning how to relate to others, accepting rules and limits—a process that takes years, continuing for many of us into adulthood.

Perhaps a way to better frame this label is to quote the *Diagnostic and Statistical Manual of Mental Disorders—Fourth Edition*, a book used extensively by psychologists and psychiatrists. It describes "Attachment Disorder of Childhood" this way:

(1) persistent failure to initiate or respond in a developmentally appropriate fashion to most social interactions, as manifest by excessively inhibited, hypervigilant, or highly ambivalent and contradictory responses (e.g., the child may respond to caregivers with a mixture of approach, avoidance, and resistance to comforting, or may exhibit frozen watchfulness).

(2) diffuse attachments as manifest by indiscriminate sociability with marked inability to exhibit appropriate selective attachments (e.g., excessive familiarity with relative strangers or lack of selectivity in choice of attachment figures).[2]

Lots of big, fancy psychological words there. To use more everyday language, RAD basically means that a child is lacking an emotional connection to significant others. The normal bonding that takes place between people, especially between child and parent, is slow in coming. Consequently, all sorts of emotional and behavior troubles can follow from this faulty core attachment.

I'm not surprised that two of the children in your adoption group are candidates for this condition. In my experience RAD is right behind oppositional defiant disorder and attention deficit hyperactivity disorder in its prevalence as a label for adoptive children, particularly those adopted later.

RAD describes a child who might be struggling to settle into a family, who is exhibiting more than expected adjustment troubles, defiance or aloofness. It offers less information about how a particular youngster may have come to be so or about his outcome someday. Reactive attachment disorder is primarily a summary term for a constellation of symptoms ranging from mild to severe.

One explanation for RAD's stretching symptoms is connected with the popularizing of the diagnosis. Here's how the phenomenon unfolds: Professionals propose a concept. It catches the media's attention, which then spread it throughout the cultural consciousness. As awareness is raised, the condition is raised in more contexts, more quickly and often prematurely.

A classic illustration of this is middle child syndrome. Most parents (especially those with an odd number of kids) can offer their understanding of MCS and how it affects a child. They might even observe how well it describes the personality of their own middle child. One small catch— there is no such syndrome. It is a "pop" disorder, promulgated by theories and the media spotlight. It captured the public's mind because it seemed to make sense, despite there being little if any research to confirm its basic tenets.

Another example, gaining momentum in the adoption world, is sensory integration disorder, a name describing a child's impaired ability to process and effectively utilize incoming sensory input. At present it's diagnosed by lots of people in lots of places. One place it's not is the diagnostic manual most relied upon by mental health professionals. Maybe someday research will more rigorously define the terms of this condition, but for now the label has gained a reality, some would say, in large part by repetition.

Am I asserting that RAD is merely a figment of our collective imagination? No. My main point is a warning: Anytime a condition gains widespread notoriety, its potential to be broadened and overused rises. RAD has a very high profile, especially in the adoption world; therefore due caution in its diagnosis is critical. Otherwise many adoptive parents, present and prospective, could be needlessly alarmed, and many adoptive kids could be prematurely labeled.

But don't some adoptive children struggle to bond with parents and siblings? Don't they need lots of time and persistent parenting to solidify an emotional connection? Of course. But remember, whatever we call the condition, we are dealing with a real child with real struggles. The name is not the answer to the problems.

Circular reasoning is another danger. Johnny is emotionally aloof and resists his parents' best efforts to socialize him. What's going on? Perhaps he has reactive attachment disorder. How did we conclude that? Because he exhibits emotional aloofness and resistance to socialization. Why does he exhibit these? Because he has RAD. We infer the diagnosis from the conduct and then explain the conduct by the label. All we did was explain in a circle.

Some years ago I was watching a television news feature about an adoptive family. The little boy, age five or so, looked quite the challenge for his parents, who were lost as to know how to handle him. Watching with a shrink's eye, I noticed any number of bad parenting and discipline habits. The dynamics between parents and preschooler were filled with loads of parental overreasoning, inconsistency and outright defeat. Near the end of the segment, the explanation for the unpleasant picture was offered: reactive attachment disorder.

Granted, I only observed several minutes of interaction. The diagnostic conclusion put forth, however, was based largely upon behavior similar to what I saw, behavior that, to be sure, was difficult. Still, it appeared that other explanations were as plausible, even more so, as some inner emotional deficit in this little five-year-old.

When RAD is proposed, it is often in the context of developmental immaturity, chaotic early life history, difficult temperament, weak parenting skills or any combination of these. In essence, the overall child-raising experience is rocky or worse. At some level, though, that is understandable, even to be expected. The child did not get a healthy, stable start. Could it be more accurate sometimes to say that the lack of attachment is due to a complex interplay of multiple factors rather than to an internal maladjustment?

Then too, a "defective" attachment may be not the cause of defective behavior but the result. If a child is hard to raise, for whatever reason, he may well be hard to relate to—in other words, to connect with. The slow attachment follows from certain personality characteristics rather than being at the root of them. Sometimes it's hard to know which came first, the tough personality or the weak bond.

Many years ago I was preparing for a possible court case in

which the question of bonding and emotional attachment had arisen. I researched several hundred related studies and articles. One clear-cut conclusion? Those children who bond least with an adult are those who have had multiple, usually short-term living arrangements, which for various reasons failed. Put another way, the more broken relationships, the harder and longer to trust a new relationship. Not a shocking finding. The reverse also followed. The younger the child when adopted, the less likely attachment troubles are to arise.

To pull together the key points: (1) reactive attachment disorder is a term that has spread rapidly into the adoption lexicon; (2) there is debate about its prevalence; (3) it is primarily a descriptive term; it tells much less about causes; (4) what is labeled RAD would sometimes better be considered a difficult, challenging parenting journey—for any combination of reasons; (5) no matter what it's called, a lack of emotional connection is best dealt with by parents willing to persevere until the connection takes shape.

chapter nine

ADOPTION OPTIONS

The book's end is nearing. I hope that my original aims were reached: Your anxieties about adoption are lessened; misconceptions are cleared up and corrected; you're thinking a little or a lot about adopting; some questions or struggles post-adoption are answered and eased.

So where do you go from here? Well, you could finish the book. After all, you've read this far.

If you're thinking a little more long-range, the questions in this chapter will introduce you to a few of the more common adoption options, as well as lower practical barriers that may lie on whichever path you're pondering. The adage says that a journey of a thousand miles begins with a single step. If you're thinking of embarking on the adoption journey, here is some guidance for your first steps.

: : :

WHO'S CALLING, PLEASE?

Dear Dr. Ray: We have two natural children. Both my wife and I have lately been feeling a tug toward adoption, but it's not really definite yet. How do people know they're called to adopt?

—*Waiting*

For many the call to adopt comes when the phone rings, and they hear of a baby or child ready for them. The internal call has been ringing steadily, as they've been childless and long ready to be child-more. In other words, for those wanting to adopt to start a family, the call is pretty clear. It's what they want, and it's been what they've wanted.

On the other hand, some couples over time feel the adoption urge fading, either because they've come to accept childlessness as a given of their existence or the years have crept up, persuading them that it's getting too late to start the whole process now. Not that they've totally ruled out the option. But any desire left would need to gain renewed strength to reopen the question. Slowly they've become more acclimated to what is, family-wise. In other words, the longer one internally debates adoption, the more likely it never happens. Inertia is a powerful force in human psychology.

Of course, adoption isn't for everybody. The great majority of folks—though the number is shrinking—are able to conceive and receive children through birth. Nonetheless, there are those—the number is growing—who begin to consider adding a child or children to their biological family through adoption. To use your words, they wonder if they are "called to adopt."

It's been my experience that many asking your question are moved by their religion. That is, at the center of their deepest held convictions is an impulse to care for others in need. Realizing all the children out there waiting for homes—for any number of race, health, age and history reasons—some veteran parents start to ponder whether they are willing and able to provide one of those homes.

This is not to say that one's motives in such cases are 100 percent altruistic. Regularly they are a mix. (Aren't most motives?) Yes, Mom and Dad want to invite another into their family. But they also may want more family, and it isn't happening through birth. Either way, the question remains, how do you know you're called? Perhaps the more precise question is, how loud does the call have to be?

For those nudged by religious beliefs, the answer is, not very loud. The idea of caring for the most vulnerable is core to their faith. They believe the Bible is the Word of God, and it tells them to take care of the widows and orphans (see James 1:27). The call is in writing; God wrote it for them.

Most Bible-based faiths would not assert that God absolutely commands adoption if one is able. Still, those who believe that the Bible speaks supernatural truth have a compelling reason to listen closely to the call, even if they aren't emotionally feeling that call so strongly yet as to prompt action.

"Are we called?" is a question that danced in Randi's and my heads for some years. We thought we had it answered several kids ago, as we mentally settled on six children as our limit. Half a dozen was a large but still manageable number, we concluded.

However, with time the itch started again, prompting us to listen once more to the adoption question. As happens regularly in my life, good words on the subject came from Randi, who essentially said, "Ray, we have a good marriage, a supportive family, a comfortable home, the finances, everything we need. If not us, who?" I hate it when she's so logical.

Granted, ten kids isn't for everybody. There are simpler ways to get tax deductions. Nevertheless, as we assessed our lives through the years, obviously with no guarantees on the future, we really had no reason to keep us from seeking to adopt another child. Fortunately for us, we kept having no reasons for the next few kids.

Whether you're thinking of expanding from none to one, one to two, two to three or nine to ten, do a little personal home study. Is your marriage solid? Is your home life a source of contentment? Are your finances manageable? Is your house able to accommodate another? Are your work schedules amenable? Are you emotionally healthy? Do you need another player for the soccer team?

Ask yourself, if you're feeling pangs to adopt, what is stopping you? Are there legitimate obstacles? Or is your uncertainty mainly founded on some vague anxiety over the unknown? Is going from what you know—and have grown comfortable with—to something you don't know the main restraint?

The fact that you are even considering adoption says that part of you wants to do this. Now you need to identify what part of you is saying not to do this. Separate the real, present-moment reasons from the *what-ifs* of whenever. Give your right-now realities more weight than those imagined or feared.

I can't count how many parents I've spoken with over the years. Among them are a large unknown number who, after their parenting days were long gone, confessed, "I wish I would have had more kids." On the other hand, I can count the number who have said to me, "I think I had too many kids. I wish I would have had one or two less." That number is zero.

:   :   :

PRETTY YOUNG FOR YOUR AGE

Dear Dr. Ray: My husband is forty-three years old, and I am forty. We're thinking of adopting. Are we too old?

—As Old as I've Ever Been

That depends upon whom you ask. A twenty-year-old would see you as one step from the nursing home's front door. A seventy-year-old thinks you're just a punk. It's all in the perspective.

If you're asking me, and you are, I have a question to ask you first: Too old for what? Competition power lifting? Yes, you're too old. Adoption? No, you're not. Most adoption agencies would agree with me. And they are the ones whose opinion really should matter to you at your age.

Of our ten children, six were adopted after I turned forty. That's not as strange as it sounds. I've made sure my much younger wife shoulders most of the child-rearing load. I do write books about it though.

Age is not the factor in adoption that it was even twenty years ago. (Twenty years ago age was probably not much of a factor for you either.) Most adoption attorneys, agencies and overseas organizations don't set the age constraints they once did. Of course, you are not fifty-three and fifty, which would reduce your options. While the age ceiling for adoption has risen, it still has some limits.

One such limit is inherent in a common adoption procedure. A birth parent, usually the mom, considers a number of prospective family profiles—pictures, history, religion, interests, anything that would offer her a summary look at possible homes for her child. Because many birth parents are age twenty or younger, they often lean toward parents near that age. Though not always.

My brother and his wife recently adopted an infant boy. His birth mom selected them because they met her main preferences for a family: stable marriage, religious foundation and "middle age" parents. My brother was thirty-nine; his wife, thirty-four. The birth mom was twenty-three. It's all in the perspective.

Your ages will have the meaning a birth parent gives to them. In my brother's case his age added to his appeal. In other cases it may not.

Adoption through an agency may involve a birth mom's input, or it may not. If the child is in the permanent custody of the agency, the birth parents, for any number of reasons, are likely no longer involved in the adoption. Whereupon it is the agency staff who judge the best placement for the child, weighing a host of variables, age of potential parents being only one.

Although the age range is more flexible than it once was, some agencies may still have age requirements linked to the laws in their state. The only way to know specifics is to research the agency.

Also, foreign governments vary widely in their views on adoptions. Again, in general age is not a major obstacle, but everything ultimately depends upon the country and its standards for adoptive parents.

Age as a question in adoption is like so many other questions: It is more or less decisive depending upon the kind of adoption pursued. A healthy infant of one's own race most often makes age, especially after forty or so, a rising hurdle. A child or children of a minority race, older, handicapped or institutionalized overall makes age less relevant.

Randi's brother and sister-in-law adopted two children from an overseas country not only quite open to U.S. adoption but with more children waiting than parents wanting. The kids were eight months and three and a half years old. My adopting relatives were fifty-eight and forty-nine.

How much of a role your age will play all comes down to the birth mom, the child, the agency and the country. Legally and logistically, you and your husband are still fairly young. But that's coming from a guy, if not one step away from the nursing home's front door, possibly pulling into the outer parking lot.

There is a level to your question beyond the numerical one. It is the physical one. "Do we have enough gas left in our tank to raise a child at this point in our lives?" I was forty-seven, my wife forty-two, when we adopted our last child, Elizabeth, at her birth. To be painfully honest, our parenting may have gotten a bit sloppier from our first to our last. Nevertheless, I believe most of our standards are still intact. Liz knows she is not allowed to smoke in the living room. Neither will she be getting a car until she's twelve, and it will be used: New Corvettes are expensive.

Advancing through parenthood for us has brought pluses and minuses. On one hand, we don't have the energy we had in raising our first children. We have to work harder to supervise, follow through and keep up. On the other hand, we are less uptight, more savvy in the ways of kids and far more practiced in discipline. We know better when to be alarmed and when something is passing kid goofiness.

All in all, my wife believes age has made us better parents. I think that's only because she's a girl. As Dad, I cling to the illusion of being able to outwrestle four of the kids at once. And I still could if they were preschoolers.

As people are marrying later in life and trying to conceive later, infertility rates are rising. Thus the average age of prospective adoptive parents is rising too. Meaning, while you and your husband are on the higher side of the age spectrum, you're not all alone somewhere off the chart. You may be creeping up there, but so are a lot of others.

In the final analysis, whether or not you are able to adopt will depend not so much upon your ages as upon your desire. Besides, you can always spin your age into a positive. On your child's first day of preschool, all the young parents will be quite impressed with you. "How sweet that you brought Oxford to school today. Grandparents have so much to offer a child."

:　:　:

PLAY IT AGAIN, MOM

Dear Dr. Ray: Our youngest of three natural children is now fifteen. My wife and I are thinking about starting over in our parenting by adopting a child, preferably over age eight. Are we out of our heads?

—*Midlife Crisis?*

Are you asking me to comment on your psychological well-being or on your inclination to adopt later in parenthood? The two could be linked, I suppose, but assuming you're emotionally stable, I'm left to opine on your post-child-raising adoption.

Though what you're thinking about doing is not common, it's not highly unusual either. As their active parenting years wind down, some people decide they're not ready for the phase-of-life shift. In the words of one mom, "I've got more mother left in me."

Of course, parents seldom ever stop being parents. My mother, even as I moved through my forties, felt compelled to ask me, "Do you have your jacket?" if the temperature dipped below sixty-five degrees, "Are you hungry?" an average of six times per visit and "Did you finish all your antibiotics?" whenever I had strep throat. Call it the natural durability of motherhood. To this day I'm grateful to her for always seeing me as her young son.

Something similar could be at work for you and your wife. Your kids better brace themselves for more of Mom and Dad's solicitousness in their adult years. Even so, it sounds as if you desire a little more direct, hands-on parenthood right now. Hence your thoughts of bringing another child into your house, one below the age of majority, that is.

What you might have lost in youthful energy you may have more than gained in veteran savvy. You've got something you didn't have years ago: experience. You've been through this parenting thing three times over. What you've learned is invaluable. Now you want to share it again. You've got the love; now you're looking for another recipient or two.

Your thinking "older child" is also the norm for older parents. One, the progression of baby to toddler to preschooler to preteen to teen may look years longer and more tiring than it did twenty-some years ago (though the number of grandparents raising grandkids is at an all-time high). Two, you've had babies. Other younger, childless couples have not. Your motives for an older child, then, may be both practical and altruistic.

Perhaps most compelling is the fact that you're in a position to adopt a harder-to-place child. You have the life skills, the parenting knowledge, the resources, the family—all of which point to a successful second go-round. In short, even if adoption was not on your radar screen when you were fully immersed in the busyness of family life, with that busyness now easing the thoughts of adoption arise.

As I noted with the last question, your age is not an obstacle, especially as you are not seeking an infant. Then too, age is not a big factor if you consider fostering first. It's quite likely that an older child would be quickly placed with you and be available to adopt in time. Whichever route you choose, adopting older would be easier for you, even if you're beyond the age range of the typical first-time adoptive parent.

What will your grown kids think about your foray into later parenthood? I can't specifically know. But I can offer a few general observations.

First, each will probably have his or her own unique perspective. Brilliant, aren't I? Their responses may vary from "That's wonderful" to "Are you nuts?" Realize, though, that whatever they think now could evolve with time. Their immediate reactions may not be reliable indicators of their eventual acceptance of your decision or of their sibling.

Second, if your children were raised by loving, stable parents—can I assume so?—the chances of their seeing warmth and wisdom in your idea rise dramatically. After all, they watched Mom and Dad's family ways for years, so they should have little trouble understanding why you want to do what you want to do. To put it succinctly, kids who are loved much are more willing to share love. I doubt you'll have to assuage much jealousy or insecurity.

Third, as clearly as you can, explain your thinking to your kids on this, making sure to elicit any and all questions they might have. Feel free to use one rationale my wife and I gave to our children as we looked to adopt again: "You guys are such great kids that we expect more of the same with other kids." Tell your children this whole idea is their fault. They made your family life so enjoyable that you can't resist doing it again.

How long will it take to adopt? Probably not very long. In my home state alone, nearly six thousand children over the age of ten are waiting for parents.

As the story goes, a little boy was walking along a starfish-littered beach, here and there throwing one back into the sea. A more "realistic" adult observed, "You can't possibly make much difference to this many starfish." The little boy answered, "Not to all of them, but to the ones I toss back, it makes all the difference in the world."

To the one you take in, it could make all the difference in his world, and it will make a big difference in yours.

: : :

FROM HERE OR THERE?

Dear Dr. Ray: My husband and I are on a waiting list to adopt a child locally. Some of our friends have adopted from overseas. Thoughts about the differences, the pros and cons?

—*To Have Kids, Will Travel*

A recent news article reported that the number of parents adopting children from abroad is soaring. In 2006 the U.S. State Department issued 20,679 visas for foreign-born adopted children. In 1990 that number was just below 7,100. Further, the figure is now very close to the total number of babies adopted from the U.S. in 2002 (22,291). More recent infant adoption comparisons aren't yet available.

Why the surge?

Some of the answer has to do with availability. Many parents wonder how long they'll be waiting to adopt, especially an infant, if they wish to do so locally. They've heard stories of couples trying for years and sometimes giving up. Given the number of countries opening their doors, even partway, to foreign adoption, there is a growing sense of having an alternative adoption route, one that could raise the probability of bringing home a little one sooner than later. I'm not aware of actual waiting time statistics for home versus foreign adoptions, but for many folks the perception is the reality. They believe more and younger children are adoptable from abroad.

Then too, when parents already are raising one or more children, they may see themselves as poor candidates to adopt stateside, barring exceptional circumstances. They gauge the chances of adding to their family as much better by heading out of the country.

Some are inclined to look abroad to minimize certain adoption anxieties. If national borders and thousands of miles are involved, there is less likelihood that a birth parent would change his or her mind and come seeking the child later. No matter that even locally the odds of an adoption reversal are remote, the media can conjure a more unsettling reality than actually is. Distance and differing cultures are seen as protective factors.

Some people believe that on the whole the percentage of children sharing wombs with drugs or alcohol is lower among foreign-born infants. So the specter of worrisome effects on the developing child doesn't loom as large. The parents feel more confident that, even if materially deprived, the child is more neurologically stable.

For others, looking like a natural family is a cultural plus. In some cases a foreign-born child may be of the same or similar race as the parents, while a local adoption may involve a child of another race, which carries the perceived pressure to establish a racial identity or to deal with others' reactions to a mixed-race family. Same-race foreign adoptions lessen, if not eliminate, these issues.

There are those whose motive to adopt from outside the country is to give a home to a youngster with minimal chance for one otherwise. Many foreign infants and children are housed in institutions with little adult contact or interaction. Sadly, most are highly unlikely to be placed anywhere else in their own countries, as local families have so few resources. Without U.S. parents open to adopting these youngsters, they would never leave the institutions until the day they were forced out because they were "too old" to be adopted or supported anymore—often while still in childhood or adolescence.

In essence, some parents are moved to adopt abroad because that is where they see the most need. They want to rescue a child, if you will. To which I say, "Good, really good."

Downsides to foreign adoptions include cost, which can sometimes top thirty thousand dollars, depending upon logistics and the requirements of the host country.

Each government can and does set its own terms for adoptions. U.S. adoptions are generally more legally standardized and less potentially complex. There are no additional requirements from a second country.

Travel can be another barrier. Many countries mandate that all parents visit the country, stay a set time and receive the child personally. Practically this can be a high hurdle, particularly for families who already have children.

Also, depending upon the child's age, there may be a more or less lengthy cultural and language transition period. Obviously most foreign countries don't speak English as a first language, so any child preschool age and up will need to learn that language here. Fortunately, young children are far more adept at this than we grown-ups are.

Because the record keeping across countries can range from pitiful to plentiful, questions of history, development and quality of care could be very difficult to answer. While the histories of some American adoptees may be known but checkered, those of foreign-born children may simply be blank. Some parents prefer even known risks to the unknown.

All in all, as it should be, every adoption is an individual matter, and what may deter some prospective parents will appeal to others. What may unsettle some will challenge others. What may give one person second thoughts will spur another to action.

Technology is shrinking the world. A smaller world opens up many more adoption options. Home or away—you've got choices. And some child somewhere is going to be the better for it.

:   :   :

Temporary to Permanent

Dear Dr. Ray: My husband and I are considering becoming foster parents with the option to adopt a child placed with us. We have mixed feelings on this. Your experience?

—*If or When?*

My experience with what is commonly called "foster to adopt" is zero—my personal experience, that is. All of our children came to us through direct adoption. Still, I've known many foster, now adoptive parents. I can offer you what I've gained through their experiences.

Foster parents are willing to open their homes and families to kids who need immediate stability, safety and comfort. They typically don't know for how long, under what conditions and, perhaps most uncertain, what the child is bringing along emotionally.

Are all foster parents angels of mercy, motivated by a selfless love for children? No. There are poor foster parents. There are a few who are more interested in the monthly stipend than the child. The human factor can misuse the most decent of ideas.

Nevertheless, my experience is that as a group, foster parents answer a unique call. It is one that asks them to adjust their life for the sake of another's life. It says, "Take in this baby, this child, this teenager, and be prepared to make his or her struggles yours." It requires them to do whatever is needed to reunite a child with birth parents if possible—to entertain parental visits, attend counseling sessions, meet with agency staff, schedule medical appointments. Sometimes foster parents have to reach much higher in their discipline repertoire to manage a youngster who gives them more challenges than any they faced with their biological children.

Beyond these fostering facts, though, lies perhaps the highest hurdle for many: the very real possibility of having to say good-bye to a child one has come to know and care about. Indeed, this provokes some of the most disconcerting questions for those pondering foster family life. They may wonder, or fear, how strongly they will emotionally attach to a child. They feel the pull to foster, but they are wary of it. On one hand is the deep impulse to be Mom and Dad, or Mom and Dad again. On the other is the worry over how they might react to watching a child leave, particularly if he will return to an environment they see as questionable.

Some people suppress the fostering impulse or let it fade completely. Their unsettledness about the future keeps them from stepping into the unknown.

How is all this relevant to you and your husband? To begin, if you decide to foster, you will quite likely encounter some temporary attachments. Many kids do indeed return to their birth home, assuming it stabilizes. If their situations again deteriorate, they may return to the foster parents, but obviously you can't know who will or when, so uncertainty lingers.

Parents who solely foster might not face quite the same sense of uncertainty, as they don't expect permanency with the children they foster. They understand their role, and this helps them accept the separations that will occur.

Parents who hope to adopt through fostering have a less defined role, as it is temporary to some and permanent to others. This requires a mindset that can take more effort to adopt, if you will.

What's the upside? Foster-to-adopt parents almost always foster to adopt. How's that? I mean, the chances of a child's needing a permanent home after all efforts to reunite have been exhausted are high. In fact, it's likely only a matter of time before you will have the opportunity to adopt, especially if the child has been with you for a time. Some bonding has already begun, and it would be most natural for it to continue permanently.

The core questions are, Are you are willing to accept the possibility that some children may live with you only for a time while others may need you for life? And can you accept the fact that you can't know at the outset which or when? If so, foster to adopt is a loving way to start your family or add to it.

While gaining your own son or daughter, you will be giving other parents and their kids a second chance. That's a great way to become a parent, if you ask me.

: : :

OPEN OR SHUT CASE

Dear Dr. Ray: The agency with which we're working is very much in favor of open adoptions. I'm nervous about the prospect. What are your opinions and experiences?

—*Afraid to Open Up*

Prior to the last fifteen or twenty years, most adoptions—other than those among family members—were closed, meaning that neither birth nor adoptive parents knew who the others were. The philosophy was that the child now had new parents and a new family, and thus it would be better for all involved to move on with life. Family relations overall would be less complicated with a clean separation from the past. Indeed, this approach guided adoption for a long time.

In the last few decades, the move toward openness, that is, establishing some contact or ongoing relationship between birth parents and the adoptive family, has accelerated. It's safe to say that it is now the dominant mind-set among adoption professionals and agencies. The rationale is that the birth mom in particular will be more comforted and settled if she is aware of who the new parents will be. What's more, any issues arising about the child's roots will be better and more sensitively managed. In essence, for everyone involved the theory says that openness is a good thing.

"Open" spans a broad continuum. Near the closed end, it may entail only an initial meeting with the birth mom, with no identities exchanged. Understandably, some birth moms wish to meet face-to-face with the parents who will love and raise their child. They seek no further contact after that.

Moving along the continuum, some type of correspondence may be requested for a period of time. The adoptive parents, for instance, may send pictures on birthdays or holidays to the agency to forward to the birth mom, with or without personal identifying information. Or contact might be in the form of regular letters or updates on the child's development, to be shared with the birth parents. These may have a clear-cut termination point, say at the child's third birthday, or last indefinitely, depending upon the initial adoption agreement.

At the more open end of the continuum are ongoing, personal contacts between the birth parents—and sometimes other family members—and the adoptive family. This is the amount of openness having the most potential to unsettle prospective adoptive parents.

Who decides how much openness? Primarily the birth mom. The agency or attorney will talk about options with her, and she will decide what corresponds to her desires for herself and the child.

The adoptive mom and dad do have a voice, however. Prior to any placement they can make known the level of openness acceptable to them and their family. In the end they and the birth parents have to agree. Essentially, both parties have to settle on the conditions.

Sometimes the birth mom, after selecting a family and hearing their preferences regarding openness, adjusts her own preferences toward theirs. Reading the family profile reassures her about who will be her baby's family, and she becomes more open to less openness.

Of our ten adoptions, eight were closed and two had some openness. The closed adoptions, several occurring twelve and more years ago, were routine at that time. Four of our children were adopted through public agencies, which had had custody of the kids for a few years; consequently the birth mother was no longer involved in any of the adoption process. The question of open or not was moot.

The birth mother of one of our younger children asked for a meeting with my wife and me, to which we readily agreed. She asked that no identities be exchanged. She simply wanted to see up close and personal the couple eager to give her child a home. We were pleased to talk with her and answer her questions, and there has been no contact since.

One of our adoptions occurred with some early openness. Randi and I were present at the birth. We know the birth mom and dad, and they know us. We have sent pictures of our child on birthdays and at Christmas. There have been only a few other personal contacts since the adoption years ago.

What is my own view of the trend toward more openness? I see pros and cons. The basic pros I've stated: They lie mainly in the sense of comfort, closure and peace for the birth mom. As to providing a broader sense of family to the child, I see less benefit. Multiple parents may sound good on paper, but real-life humans can complicate the best-laid intentions.

I am most cautious about the idea of ongoing personal contacts. While wide openness may look ideal, reality is usually less smooth. Will the biological mom continue to be comfortable, even agreeable, to the arrangement? Will she want increasing contact over time? Could dramatic changes in her life shift her initial feelings and motives?

As a psychologist I hear every day of the emotional ebbs and flows of life common to all of us. Birth moms, especially younger ones, likely will experience many unforeseen changes and stresses in their next ten to twenty years. It is those changes that can impact the adoptive family and its sense of stability.

What about any other children of the birth mom, now or in the future? Will they be included in visitations? At what level?

Are there other adopted children in the adoptive family? How will they react to the situation? What thoughts and feelings will contacts foster in them regarding their own circumstances?

Medical history is another matter. Most of the time this information is available and is shared with adoptive parents. Also, should medical problems arise for the adoptee, biological family information can generally be obtained and shared.

As is so in virtually every other aspect of our existence, technology is dramatically changing the "open versus closed" adoption question. With only the slightest bits of identifying information, birth parents or adoptive children when age-capable can begin an Internet search leading to any person and their locale, along with uncovering other pieces of life information. This is even more possible with children adopted older, who may know names, places and assorted history about their earlier years.

A few general cautions may help lower the chances of a child's using technology to seek birth parents before she is emotionally ready, or of a birth parent's seeking you or the child unexpectedly:

- Except for the most unusual reasons, allow no computer in a child's bedroom; keep it where you can easily oversee its use. Passwords to get online and good screening programs are a must.
- If your youngster had a Social Security number at the time of adoption, get a new one. Any person who knows that number can easily use it to locate your child, access private information or, in the extreme case, steal an identity. It's best to eliminate as many points of unwanted or intrusive contact as possible.

To pull it all together, my position on openness is somewhat more cautious than the conventional thinking. Be it due to years of counseling, others' adoption stories or my own personal experience, my sense is that the more open, the more potential for unanticipated, very human complications.

:   :   :

THE COST FACTOR

Dear Dr. Ray: Our hearts are willing, but our wallet is weak. We may be able to pay for one adoption, but more than that and we'd have to sell our house and move into a camper.

—*Low-Money Mommy*

The cost of an adoption is a highly variable thing. It can range from zero to forty thousand dollars, here and there more. Why such a spread? Because of the spread of factors involved. Here are just a few of the basic questions affecting the financial picture:

- Who will you be working with—a private attorney or an agency? A public agency or a private one? Religious or secular?
- Do you wish to adopt one child or a sibling group? Healthy infant or youngster with special needs? Your race or another?
- Are you looking to adopt in the U.S. or from another country? Which country?
- Will you foster parent first?

When all is said and paid, adoption costs generally run between fifteen thousand and twenty-five thousand dollars, though I must qualify. Typically this sum covers an infant adopted privately through an attorney or agency. If you are planning to adopt a child with special needs, then you will not only wait less but most likely pay less. Why so is beyond the scope of this book. Let it just be said that even though all children are equal in value, they are not equal in cost.

Even with all else being equal, for most folks a price near zero has more appeal than one flirting with thirty thousand dollars. No-cost adoptions are not uncommon. They are done almost exclusively by public agencies, generally at the county or state level. Because these agencies are funded by public monies for the care of children, they absorb the fees involved from beginning to end of the adoption process. The children tend to be older, though infants are available, or they present some "special needs." Recall, though, the flexibility of that term.

Four of our children were adopted through county agencies at ages two, three, four and four. We incurred no expenses at all, unless you tally my wife's coffee tab and phone bill to her mother as she was raising six kids, ages six and under, not counting me.

Out of the public sphere, costs vary more widely, contingent upon what any attorney, agency, county or state requires in the way of assessment, background checks, profiling, medical screening, birth mother and baby support and so on. Many procedures, and thus costs, are mandated by law. Sometimes additional expenses occur, such as counseling, living expenses for the birth mom, hospital care, temporary foster care and travel. The final financial tally depends upon the individual circumstances of the adoption.

Private adoption is where prospective parents can get most nervous about finances, though agencies and attorneys are pretty accurate in giving an estimate of the end figures. It isn't that parents are reluctant to absorb what is basically the price of a new car; they're concerned about their lack of control over its options—the unknowns, if you will. Or like you, they hope to someday adopt another child, and they are anxious about mounting debt.

The government to the rescue! (Now, that's a phrase you don't hear in too many venues.) Currently the IRS offers an adoption tax credit covering up to ten thousand dollars of the adoption expenses per child. Because this is a credit, not a deduction, you will get back the federal taxes you pay in the adoption year and the next two years, if need be, to recoup the full ten thousand dollars. While this may not cover all adoption costs, it is a nice-sized rebate. You will need the proof-of-purchase seal.

Also, to help cover any unique expenses involved in raising a special needs youngster, you could be eligible for a monthly stipend provided by the local agency, the state or Social Security until the child is eighteen. A determination of that stipend is made early in the adoption process.

So even though the cost of an adoption can sound formidable, like the cost of one year of college or, worse, preschool, there are funds to reduce the outlay. Who knows, perhaps enough so that if you adopt a second child, you can afford a really big camper.

: : :

First Steps, at Last

Dear Dr. Ray: We've decided to adopt. Where do we begin?

—*Ready*

A whole book could be devoted to your question. The legalities and logistics of adoption depend much on the who, what, when, where and why of it all. Previous questions throughout this book touched upon a range of adoption options, so now we'll pull together some basics to help get you started.

Option one: a private attorney. Though any attorney can legally oversee an adoption, there are those who specialize in adoptions. They are intimately familiar with the laws and procedures in their states. They have lists of prospective parents and can estimate for you the waiting time. Most adoption attorneys will confirm that the more open you are to children of another race or those with special needs, the shorter your wait.

A good first contact with attorneys is via a letter introducing yourself, your interest in adoption, your history and any other details you believe relevant. You can write to one or to one thousand. Prior to our first adoption, my wife and I mailed a one-page letter to several hundred attorneys. A number of them responded, and ironically our first son came through one who had never done an adoption.

If you choose to go with a private attorney, seek those not only in your area but in other states, who would welcome your interest. How do you find them? The American Bar Association, the Internet, state organizations, word of mouth, other adoptive parents' contacts.

Option two: an agency. Most adoptions occur through agencies of two types—private or nonprofit and public. The general policies and conditions among agencies are fairly similar, with some variances in particulars. The fees vary, with the public agency costing less, often minimal or nothing. Agencies also differ greatly in available children, their races, needs and ages. Some predominantly place infants; others, older children.

An invaluable resource for evaluating agencies, their procedures and specialty areas is the *Adoption Resource Handbook*. Available in the reference section of your local library, it lists agencies by state, offering plenty of useful information about each.

Agencies routinely offer basic information about available children on the Internet. For instance, if you search "Adoption—Ohio," you will be directed to a Web site that identifies children waiting for adoption in agencies across that state. Type again, say, "Female below age ten," and these children will be grouped. Most people are stunned at how many kids are waiting for parents.

Agencies and attorneys often work together to more smoothly expedite an adoption or to better manage its details. In fact, cooperation across agencies, attorneys and countries is standard practice.

Of our ten children, three were adopted through private attorneys, two through private agencies, one through an attorney-agency cooperation and four through county government agencies. Increasing your adoption chances and decreasing your waiting period involve doing some homework first, finding out who and what is the best fit for your goals and hopes.

Option three: foreign country. The number of foreign adoptions has jumped dramatically in recent years. More countries are opening their doors to U.S. adoptions. The children, requirements, fees and visitation conditions differ from country to country, sometimes dramatically so. One country may erect hurdles that will stall all but the most determined. Another will almost deliver the child to you. Commonly agencies, domestic or overseas, will manage the whole process. Again, some preliminary legwork will help you identify agencies and countries most compatible with your intentions.

Option four: foster to adopt. A previous question in this chapter, "Temporary to Permanent," dealt with this adoption pathway, so we won't revisit the subject here. If you can tolerate some uncertainty on your road to parenthood, this option almost always leads to children, sometimes several.

Option five: good fortune, good timing, God's providence. All these can enter any adoption mix. As I've shared, with our first son the attorney was about to retire, had never done an adoption, was unsure what to do with our letter and probably was getting ready to discard it when a colleague walked down the hall, poked his head in the door and asked, "Do you know anyone who might want to adopt?"

As an aside, the evening prior to our first meeting with the attorney, I took a finger in the eye playing basketball and was fitted at the emergency room with a temporary eye patch. My wife, after seeing I was all right, was ready to hit me in the other eye. I've always suspected that had she had a few days, she would have found a husband stand-in for at least that initial interview. After all, we both had those first-time-adoption jitters over making a positive impression. Imagine my relief when we saw that the attorney wore an eye patch. Well, not really, but he did like basketball.

Sometimes a young mother seeks to place her baby for adoption, and she wants either to know the adoptive family personally or be connected with them through her social circle. Let your family, friends, acquaintances and physicians know of your desire to adopt. They might become aware of a situation in which the birth mom has unique conditions for adoption, and you might fit them.

Attorneys ultimately have to be involved to help navigate the legalities from start to finish. But I've heard many happy-ending adoption stories in which a friend knew a friend who knew a young mother who wished to find her own adoptive family.

One of our children came to us in this way. A birth grandparent asked our help in locating prospective parents for a very young pregnant girl's child. She did not wish to use agencies or attorneys until necessary. As we searched, along the way she decided to ask us to adopt the baby. At the time we weren't actively looking to adopt, so we were surprised but grateful for the opportunity. I guess you could say we experienced our first unplanned adoption. We're so glad we never practiced "safe phone."

I've summarized only a brief series of options. Once you sort through how and where you want to start, the adoption folks involved will guide you the rest of the way. You'll learn much as you go and even more after you adopt. And if you adopt more than once, your familiarity with all this will grow exponentially.

Then, who knows, you might be able to write your own adoption book.

: : : n o t e s : : :

CHAPTER SIX: COMMUNICATION 101

1. Corrie Ten Boom with John and Elizabeth Sherrill, *The Hiding Place* (Old Tappan, N.J.: Spire, 1971), pp. 26–27.

CHAPTER SEVEN: ADOPTION SELF-IMAGE: MYTHS AND TRUTHS

1. See, for example, *Discipline That Lasts a Lifetime: The Best Gift You Can Give Your Kids* (Cincinnati: Servant, 2003) and *Good Discipline, Great Teens* (Cincinnati: Servant, 2007).

CHAPTER EIGHT: ADOPTION DISCIPLINE BASICS

1. Raymond N. Guarendi, *You're A Better Parent Than You Think! A Guide to Common-Sense Parenting* (New York: Fireside, 1992), pp. 115–116.

2. *Diagnostic and Statistical Manual of Mental Disorders, Fourth Edition* (Washington, D.C.: American Psychiatric Association, 1994), p. 118.